WORD PROCESSORS AND THE WRITING PROCESS

An Annotated Bibliography

Compiled by
PAULA REED NANCARROW,
DONALD ROSS,
and
LILLIAN BRIDWELL
with
Max Fritzler, Technical Consultant

Greenwood Press
Westport, Connecticut • London, England

Library of Congress Cataloging in Publication Data

Nancarrow, Paula Reed.
  Word processors and the writing process.

  Includes index.
    1. English language—Rhetoric—Study and teaching—
Bibliography.   2. Word processing—Bibliography.
3. Authorship—Data processing—Bibliography.   I. Ross,
Donald.   II. Bridwell, Lillian S.   III. Title.
Z5818.E5N35   1984   [PE1404]   016.808'042'028   83-22749
ISBN 0-313-23995-9 (lib. bdg.)

Library of Congress Catalog Card Number: 83-22749
ISBN: 0-313-23995-9

First published in 1984

Greenwood Press
A division of Congressional Information Service, Inc.
88 Post Road West, Westport, Connecticut 06881

Printed in the United States of America

10 9 8 7 6 5 4 3 2 1

Contents

Preface

This bibliography represents our efforts to bring together all the information available to us on a single question: What information might help those who are interested in the ways computers can help writers, especially university students, with the art and craft of writing? When we first began the search, in a graduate seminar at the University of Minnesota in 1981, we were discouraged because we found so little that was directly relevant to the question, but over the last two years, the information explosion has finally rocked the writing world. We have barely been able to keep up with the new journals springing up devoted to the topic, much less with all of the conferences, papers, articles, and books that deal with computers and writing. We believe, however, that this bibliography provides, in a single place, a comprehensive listing of the major resources and enough references to lead those who will use it to the most promising areas for new developments.

In our annotations we have tried to amplify the titles of our sources to give the reader a sense of the topics they include. Our index terms, listed below the annotations, should also help to guide the reader who is interested in more specific questions. By no means do our index terms account for all that may be included in a particular source, but they do describe the issues we judge to be of greatest interest to those who teach writing. We hope that the listing of index terms with the annotations will make it easy for users of the index to locate the relevant citation or citations on the page in question.

When we have stated or implied a criticism, it generally stems from our concern that writing instruction should be informed by the best available empirical data on writing and learning and by current theories from rhetoric, cognitive psychology, linguistics, and other fields. We do not believe that writing instruction can stop with the correction of surface mistakes, and so we urge future researchers and system developers to take a broad and intellectually rich view of the students and teachers for whom they work.

If our criticisms reflect our ignorance of the most recent computer technologies or computer science theories, we beg indulgence because we are writing teachers first and computer specialists only in an applied way. We have accepted the obligation to educate ourselves about computer technology, however, because we believe most strongly that humanists must make themselves heard if computers are to be used in principled and theoretically sound ways in the writer's world.

We have consciously avoided the temptation to present a comprehensive survey of the hardware (computing machines) or software (the programs that make computers work) which are available to writers. Cheaper and better equipment and programs appear weekly, so we have tried to take a broad view, reviewing only those hardware developments that represent new possibilities for writers and only those programs that represent major contributions to writers or that suggest areas for future research. This broader view is also necessary because so many computer programs are designed to run only on specific machines. Current information of this sort can be found in such publications as BYTE, Creative Computing, InfoWorld, and Computer and Control

PREFACE

Abstracts, as well as in publications from such sources as Datapro Research. Finally, we avoided reviews of many programs because much of what is currently available does not meet our standards for a "broad and intellectually rich" view of what computers should do for students of writing. With the exception of word processing packages, which are the best of what is available for writers, the promise is often greater than the reality in the software world of 1983.

For practical purposes, if one is a college or university teacher or administrator faced with the task of acquiring computers and software for writing, one must study the market very cautiously to make wise decisions. The wide technological gulf between the writing teacher and the computer salesperson creates a lucrative market for "snake oil peddlers." We highly recommend that these decisions be made in consultation with unbiased experts in computer centers or computer science departments.

Further, we must trust our judgments about what it takes to teach people to write well. The computer is not a panacea, but rather a new powerful tool. It makes some things easier--correcting spelling errors, adding information to a manuscript, preparing polished copy--but it cannot read and it cannot write. Neither can it decide what a student needs to know to learn to write. Writing teachers can be confident that they are still the best judges of what is useful and what is not, on or off the computer. We trust that our annotations reflect our own criteria for making these judgments.

We have consciously thought about the issues raised in F. W. Lancaster's intriguing work, Toward Paperless Information Systems (1978), especially his ideas in chapter five of that book. We know that the contexts for written language will be radically different as communications systems change the ways we produce and exchange information. To a great degree, this bibliography represents the future. By having sought out and included working papers from both computer companies and academic researchers, we believe our coverage is a bit ahead of what is currently being published in most writing journals. We have listed a few books and a fair number of papers that are "in press" or "unpublished manuscripts," especially when we have good evidence that they will eventually emerge in print (or on a data base). Of course, some of these may fail to materialize, but we have included them to alert those who use this bibliography to people and places from which future developments are likely to occur.

In several places we have noted "old" articles, that is, those published in 1975 or before, with a brief comment on their age. We felt that it was important to represent some of the history in this new field. If a source had no further trace in the literature, we have assumed that the project was abandoned for some reason. Nearly all projects reported on before about 1980 involved "batch" computing, which means that the "input" to the computer, usually a large "mainframe" computer, was through cards, and the "output" was a regular 11 X 14" printout of results. Early studies often involved "key punching" students' essays onto cards and then analyzing them according to some linguistic methodology. They generally produced statistical information about secondary measures of writing, for example, counts of text features and raters' scores. We have not tried to cover these projects systematically, as they were undertaken in a

PREFACE

computing environment far different from the microcomputer world in which even elementary school children can directly compose on a computer screen and immediately print out their writing.

In a very few cases, we have retained citations that are clearly unrelated to our question. We could have pressed a few keys and eliminated them forever, but we thought it might save others time to find, through our annotations, that an appealing title was misleading.

Some readers may think that we have included too many references on spelling checkers, readability programs, syntactic programs, and pattern-practice packages, particularly as we see them as peripheral to the needs of college students who are learning the more complex skills of writing. To some degree, our coverage reflects what has been done with computers, and as the computer is well-suited to analyze these surface issues, much work has been done in these areas.

In addition to the bibliography proper and the index, we have provided a directory of "Relevant Journals," selectively annotated as to their usefulness, and a glossary of pertinent generic terms, trade names and acronyms.

With all our caveats behind us, we admit that we have been bitten by the computer bug. We find ourselves frustrated as writers when we don't have access to them. Indeed, we probably would not have had the time and resources to maintain such an exhaustive compilation without our trusty word processing packages. They made adding new entries possible without ever retyping. The index appeared miraculously with new page numbers at the end of each version every time we printed it. Our publisher was able to use camera-ready copy direct from our computer's laser printer.

In addition to thanking our WordStar and Final Word software, and our Xerox and VAX computers, we must take time to remember the people who did what computers cannot do: read, write, think, and program the all too literal and stubborn computers. Robert Brooke, Steve Brehe, Steve Deyo, Nancy Stone, and Gerry Wasiluk read and commented on many of the references we have included. Colleagues around the country read early versions and pointed out omissions. Others heard of our project and risked sending us their "cutting edge" work. We dare not begin to mention names, but their work is in the bibliography and we thank them.

Elaine Collins from the University of Minnesota Computer Center helped us understand the computers' literal ways. She showed us how to match our intentions with formatting commands so that the printed versions began to resemble our visions.

Max Fritzler, Technical Consultant to the project, immersed himself in the idiosyncrasies of text processing packages and our computers; he was the one among us who knew enough to converse with Elaine about all the technicalities. Max had the patience to stay with us as we changed our minds about margins, bibliographical styles, and countless wordings. It was he who emerged with the final printed version and he

PREFACE

who earned the t—shirt emblazoned with "Born to Hack." Some may know him for his work in Philosophy as he finishes his Ph.D, but we know him as a computer expert.

Financial support for our work came from grants from the University of Minnesota's Educational Development Program and from the Fund for the Improvement of Postsecondary Education. Neither the University nor the Fund is responsible for the accuracy of the listings or the opinions expressed; the compilers take full responsibility for these.

Finally, we appreciate Marilyn Brownstein's cooperation at Greenwood Press. She believed in the timeliness of the information we had gathered and worked with us to publish it using our new technologies.

P.R.N.
D.R.
L.S.B.

September 1983

Abbreviations

We here list abbreviations used as part of the title of the journal or published proceedings. Please consult the glossary for other abbreviations, especially those which abbreviate technical terms or phrases, such as CPU.

ACM Association of Computing Machinery

ADCIS Association for the Development of Computer–Based Instructional Systems.

AEDS Association for Educational Data Systems

AFIPS American Federation of Information Processing Societies

ALLC Association for Literary and Linguistic Computing

ASIS American Society of Information Science

CIPS Canadian Information Processing Society

IEEE Institute of Electrical and Electronics Engineers

IFIP International Federation for Information Processing

IUCC Inter–University Committee on Computing

NCTE National Council of Teachers of English

NTIS National Technical Information Service

PARC Palo Alto Research Center (Xerox, Inc.)

THE BIBLIOGRAPHY

Adam, T. L., Aiken, J. A., Jr., Herbert, R. A., Herzik, A. M., Levine, L. J., & White, F. R. (1982). Screen scrolling. IBM Technical Disclosure Bulletin, 24(8), 4125-6.

Discusses effects of vertical scrolling in a keyboard/display word processing system.
[Design of Software]

Ager, D. E., Knowles, F. E., & Smith, J. (Eds.). (1979). Modular programs for individual researchers unfamiliar with computers. Advances in computer-aided literary and linguistic research. Birmingham, UK: Department of Modern Languages, University of Aston.

Aiken, R. M. (1981). The golden rule and ten commandments of computer based education (CBE). T. H. E. Journal, 8(3), 39-42.
[Computer Aided Instruction]

Alberga, C. N. (1967). String similarity and misspellings. Communications of the ACM, 10, 302-313.
[Spelling Checkers]

Alcock, B. G. (1979). English strands: A status report. In Proceedings of the Association for Educational Data Systems, 17th Annual Conference, Detroit, MI (Washington, D.C.: Association for Educational Data Systems), 12-14.

Describes a series of computerized English drill programs. Assumes computerized drills, organized in strands, can supplement teacher's curriculum and save time. A student recordkeeping system is also involved.
[Computer Aided Instruction]

All about 90 word processing software packages. (1981). Datapro Research, 1805 Underwood Blvd., Delram, NJ 08075, 52 pp.

Provides information on vendors, computer models, processing and operating system requirements, source language or compiler, availability of source listing, training, maintenance, documentation, price, and number of users. Ninety packages reviewed from seventy-three vendors.
[Survey of Software]

Allee, J. C. (1979). English usage exercises II: A CAI series for the elementary school. In Proceedings of Association for Educational Data Systems, 17th Annual Conference, Detroit, MI (Washington, DC: Association for Educational Data Systems), 15-18.

Describes EUX II, a series of computerized grammar lessons and exercises for use at terminals (not stand-alone micros). EUX II is designed for intermediate

elementary students, and each exercise session takes about 10-12 minutes. Article says it's available for the cost of handling, but note the date.
[EUX]

Allee, J. G., & Williams, R. L. (1980). The pedagogical use of interrogative sentences in language arts CAI. Computer-based instruction: A new decade. 1980 Conference Proceedings (pp. 55-61). Bellingham, WA: Association for the Development of Computer-Based Instructional Systems.

> Claims that interrogative sentence forms are good tools for CAI grammar programs.
> [Design of Software, Computer Aided Instruction, Grammar Drill]

Allen, T., Nix, R., & Perlis, A. (1981). Pen: A hierarchical document editor. In Proceedings of the ACM SIGPLAN (pp. 74-81).

> PEN uses a hierarchical model of document structure, similar to SCRIBE, to format the text, rather than making the user specify large amounts of formatting information. What is of interest about SCRIBE and PEN is their reliance on "tree-structures," complete with nodes which divide up the document into chapters, sections, quotations, descriptions, etc. PEN's formatting power, according to this article, however, "is not accessible while developing a document; it is available only after a compilation." But the existing system, which rigidly defines how its nodes may be subdivided, would probably make a paltry heuristic. Touches briefly upon the advantages of the display window for accessing inter- and intra-document references while reading a particular text on the screen. See also Barach.
> [PEN, SCRIBE]

Anandam, K., et al. (1979). RSVP: Feedback program for individualized analysis of writing. New York: Exxon Education Foundation Research Report. (ERIC Document Reproduction Service No. ED 191 511)

> Describes in more detail the experimental study discussed above. Anandam's operating principle, that "what has been needed" in computer-assisted instruction in English is "a computer-assisted program that becomes an integral part of the total instructional effort, affecting and being affected by the faculty who use it" is a good one; it makes for a major distinction between RSVP and most other text feedback programs. The instructor reads the essay first and selects no more than five errors for computer prescriptions, rather than having the computer scan for patterns and problems and spit out a ton of overwhelming information. The instructor then may include her own written comments as well. The program uses punch cards, however, which micro-oriented folks might find unfamilar and tedious. (For an alternative, see William Marling's description of his WRITER/GRADER/READER software package, which unites a grading system and a micro-based word processor, below.) RSVP is written in FORTRAN. The

feedback is at seventh, ninth and eleventh grade reading levels; many of the developmental/remedial instructors thought that an even more basic level than seventh grade was needed for some of their students. The attitude questionnaires for faculty and students given at the end of the term provide useful and interesting information, though the discussion section contains a few weak speculations. See also RSVP manual, listed as such.
[RSVP]

Anandam, K., Eisel, E., & Kotler, L. (1980). Effectiveness of a computer-based feedback system for writing. Journal of Computer-Based Instruction, 6(4), 125-133.

Describes how RSVP, a computer-based instructional management system for freshman composition at Miami-Dade Community College, was employed in an experimental study. RSVP (Response System for Variable Prescriptions) helps teachers give students individualized feedback on common, handbook-style writing errors and also works as a recordkeeping system, not just for grades but for student writing and instructor feedback. RSVP is intended to be a teacher support system; it allows teachers individualized control over their curriculum and does not prescribe what materials to use, how to teach or what the grades must be. Results of one experiment show that RSVP students did significantly better on an objective test at the end of the course than non-RSVP students.
[RSVP]

Anandam, K., & Kelly, J. T. (1982). Teaching and technology: Closing the gap. T. H. E Journal, 10, 84-90.

Discusses the large discrepancy between current sophisticated applications of communications technology in "the world" and the meager use of such technology in educational circles; urges faculty to use their ingenuity to exploit technology for pedagogical purposes.

Anandan, P., Embley, D. W., & Nagy, G. (1980). An application of file-comparison algorithms to the study of program editors. International Journal of Man-Machine Studies, 13, 201-11.

As stated in the title, the chief focus is on the editing of computer programs. In the face of a large number of editing systems, how can one judge among them? The algorithm compares two versions of the same text, looking for identical or similar matches, and for deleted or new strings. Obvious problems arise when parts of the text are moved, or when deletions or additions are large. Given the space required (500K) and the need to use a large computer, this approach does not seem fruitful for comparing versions of a text in natural language.
[Design of Software]

Anderson, C. W., & McMaster, G. E. (1982). Computer assisted modeling of affective tone in written documents. <u>Computers and the Humanities</u>, <u>16</u>, 1–9.

Describes a computer program, PSA (Psychological Semantic Analysis) intended "to assist in the analysis and modeling of emotional tone in text" (p. 1). As a tool for the content analysis of literature, the program goes to a lot of trouble to "objectively measure" how emotionally loaded a text is; a program which can detect that chapter 2 of Joyce Carol Oates' <u>Wonderland</u> is very disturbing seems a small gain, even a redundancy, though the resulting "tension graph" which is produced is interesting in showing verbal patterns of tension in a visual form.

More significant for student writing was the analysis of 58 student papers describing a hypothetical "best" and "worst" future career scenario. Predictably, the degree of positive tone in the "best" career situation was higher than that of "worst" careers: "desirable future careers were conceived of as more energetic and active than undesirable futures." "Worst" future descriptions were negative and passive. As a prototype for a tool for student writers who have difficulty perceiving a lack of objectivity in their own writing, or in reading they must respond to, the program may have some merits.
[Semantics]

Annet, J., & Duke, J. (Eds.). (1970). In <u>Proceedings of a seminar on computer based learning systems</u>. London: National Council for Educational Technology.
[Computer Aided Instruction]

Antista, J. H. (1974). <u>A comparative study of computer–assisted and non–computer–assisted instruction in senior high school English classes</u>. Ph.D. thesis. Wayne State University, 1974. <u>Dissertation Abstracts International</u> <u>35</u>(12–A) (1975), 7600.

Studied the effects on senior high school students' performance and attitudes toward computer aided instruction used to teach basic English grammar. During 1970–1971, four classes of "average" students were divided into two experimental (one male, one female) and two control (one male, one female) groups; the experimental used CAI, while the control did not. The same three teachers worked with all four groups. Pre–tests and post–tests were given and data were analyzed for statistical significance. There was no significant difference between the experimental and control groups in the areas of language arts achievement, study habits/attitudes/orientation, attitudes towards education in general or English class in particular, or in school–related areas of self–concept and motivation. Within the experimental groups however, there was a significant difference in achievement between those who used the computer ten or fewer times and those who used it eleven or more times. Recommendations for future CAI use and development and suggestions for further research are outlined.
[Computer Aided Instruction, Case Study]

Appleby, B. C. (1983). Computers and composition: An overview. <u>Focus: Teaching English Language Arts</u>, <u>9</u>(3), 102–110.

A general argument for computers in writing classes, including a brief discussion of the future developments we can expect. Appleby has also compiled an introductory bibliography, "A Bibliographic Guide for Beginners on Computers and Composition," printed in this special issue of Focus, published by the Southeastern Ohio Council of Teachers of English and Ohio University's Department of English Language and Literature.
[Bibliography]

Arlette, V. (1976). Computer "co-authors" book. Canadian Datasystems, 8(2), 46-7.

Not applicable, and dated. Describes the use of a computer to revise, edit and phototypeset a book on Sartre. Anecdotal.
[Testimonial]

Arms, V. M. (1983). The computer and the process of composition. Pipeline, 8(1), 16-18.

Brief descriptions of the programs Arms has developed at Drexel University: CREATE (modeled after H. Burns' work on invention), FORMAT (focuses attention on various parts of a report the student is preparing and provides surface feedback), and EDITOR (allows for easy revision on the screen). She also describes the positive benefits her students perceived in technical writing courses.
[INVENT]

Arms. V. (1983). The computer kids and composition. (ERIC Document Reproduction Service No. ED CS 207 052)

Armstrong. (1980). Unintelligible management resumes and academic prestige. Interfaces, 10(2), 80-86.

Asimov, I. The word processor and I. Popular Computing, February 1982, 1(4), 32-4.

Asimov, of science fiction fame, is a well-known endorser of word processors for writing. Anecdotal.
[Testimonial]

Baker, F. B. (1978). Computer managed instruction: Theory and practice. Englewood Cliffs, NJ: Education Technology Publications.

Not specifically on computer-assisted writing instruction, but provides general recommendations which might be useful.
[Computer Aided Instruction]

Baker, J. D., & Goldstein, I. (1966). Batch vs. sequential displays: Effects on human problem solving. Human Factors, 8, 225-235.

    [Human Factors]

Bailey, R. W. (1974). Computer-assisted poetry: The writing machine is for everybody. In J. L. Mitchell (Ed.), Computers in the Humanities. Edinburgh: Univ. of Edinburgh Press, 283-295.

    Review article with a rather complete list of readings about computer-produced poetry. A fine place to start.

    [Poetry Writing, Bibliography]

Barach, D. R., Taenzer, D. H., & Wells, R. E. Design of the PEN Video Editor Display Module. Proceedings of the ACM SIGPLAN/SIGOA Symposium on Text Manipulation, June 1981.

    Technical article on software design, especially software to manipulate the screen. See Allen, et al., above.

    [PEN, Design of Software]

Barth, R. J. (1979). An annotated bibliography of readings for the computer and the English teacher. English Journal, 68(1), 88-92.

    [Bibliography]

Barton, B. F. & Barton, M. S. (1983). Communication models for computer-mediated information systems: The role of the technical-communication specialist. Paper given at the Annual Convention on College Composition and Communication, Detroit, and available from the authors at the Department of Humanities, University of Michigan, Ann Arbor, MI 48109.

    Surveys the failure of technical-communication specialists to be interested in or involved in designing or even commenting on information systems. While the communication specialists may have been alienated by the arcana of large computers which were only controlled by computer experts, the situation is changing rapidly. Smaller and more independent computers, and changing philosophies of business management should be more hospitable to positive and assertive statements about what communication can and should be.

    [Communication Systems]

Bates, M., et al. (1981) Generative tutorial systems. In 1981 Conference Proceedings, ADCIS, Association for the Development of Computer-Based Instructional Systems (pp. 12-21). Western Washington University.

    [Computer Aided Instruction]

Bath, P. (1982) Making use of word power. Micro Decision, 6, 49-50.

Reviews word processing program called THE WORD for CP/M.
[THE WORD]

Beam, P. (1978). COMIT English module. In Symposium on COMIT. Waterloo, Ontario, Canada. (ERIC Document Reproduction Service No. ED 167 189)

Describes a multi-media (including computers) approach to analyzing a poem.
[COMIT] [Literary Analysis]

Bean, J. C. (1983). Computerized word-processing as an aid to revision. College Composition and Communication, 34, 146-148.

Very brief, anecdotal report of successes at Montana State University. The usual claims for ease of revision.
[Testimonial]

Beechhold, H. G. (1983). People and computers: An English course. Collegiate Microcomputer, 1, 149-151.

A personal account of an informal, two-week introduction to computers which the author teaches regularly in an English Department. In "People and Computers" he offers easy access to computers and discusses the following topics: the machine, types of software, experiments in programming (student exposure), solving problems with computers (standard commercial packages), problems caused by computers, the computer and society, and how to buy a personal computer.
[Testimonial]

Behrens, L. & Stern F. J. (1983). Essaywriter: A textbook-software package for writing courses. Unpublished manuscript. Systematics General Corporation, 18327 Allspice Dr., Germantown, MD 20874, 51 pp.

A textbook proposal which strives to go beyond drill-based lessons. The proposed programs go through the stages of the "classic" term paper, from note cards through revision. The programs are to be written in BASIC for a TRS-80 microcomputer, and will be directed at a secondary school audience. One way of analyzing students' prewriting is to limit the essay to prescribed reading topics. The revision programs follow the lines set out by R. Lanham's Revising Business Prose (and the UCLA implementation of the same ideas in the HOMER program).
[HOMER]

Bell, K. (1980). The computer and the English classroom. English Journal, 69, 88-90.

A very basic consumers' guide to microcomputers for high school educators interested in obtaining and programming them for classroom instruction. Of use only to the reader who needs the most rudimentary knowledge.

[Survey]

Belmore, N. F. (1975). Language teaching research and the computer. Technical Report, Swedish Council for Social Science Research, October.

Bender, T. K. (1975). A literary text conceived in a data bank. Proceedings of the 38th ASIS Annual Meeting Information Revolution, Boston, Mass. (pp. 82-83). Washington, DC. American Society of Information Science.

> Paper describes preparation of the complete works of Joseph Conrad for computer analysis.
> [Literary Analysis]

Bender, T. K. (1976). Literary texts in electronic storage: The editorial potential. Computers and the Humanities, 10. 193-199.

> Bender presents a notion of the literary work as being a dynamic summary of all its editions, the author's manuscript(s), notes, and so on. He directly contradicts the theory in textual editing that the last version the author saw is the "real" text, reflecting her or his "real" intentions. To deal with the complexity of the dynamic text, Bender proposes a computer-based text manager. The parallels with seeing student writing as a dynamic process are obvious, and Bender's hypothetical solution may prove to be enormously fruitful.
> [Literary Analysis]

Bennett, J. L. (1972). The user interface in interactive systems. In C. A. Cuadra (Ed.), Annual Review of Information Science and Technology, 7. American Society for Information Science, Washington, 159-196.

> [Human Factors]

Bennett, J. L. (1979). The commercial impact of usability in interactive systems. Man/Computer Communication, 2. Infotech State of the Art Report, Maidenhead, England, 1-17.

> [Human Factors]

Berkeley, E. C. (1980). Writing a novel by computer--Part 4: Events. Computers and People. 29(2), 20-24.

Berman, P., & Wasser, A. (1978). New technology and the technical author. Technical Communication, 25(3), 2-7.

> Notices that commercial word- and text-processing systems were built for the secretary and publisher, respectively, rather than the author. Military systems are

- 8 -

user-oriented, so again, the author is left out. The bulk of the article is on then-recent developments, e.g., moving to stand alone minicomputers, and criteria for selecting a system. The authors don't say what an author-oriented system would look like.

Berry, E. (1982). Writing with a word processor for scholars, poets and freshmen. Paper presented at the Modern Language Association Annual Convention, Los Angeles.

A readable introductory piece about the potential of word processors for writing. Cites Asimov as well as several other testimonials of the popular computer journal variety, and integrates these sources with solid composition folk (Shaughnessy, Bazerman, Elbow, Lanham, etc.). Berry's experience has been that word processor's writing fluidity transfers to other forms of writing when students are deprived of the machine, but her sample of writers is relatively small, and she relies a great deal on her own experience with the machine. On the whole, an enthusiastic testimonial, but more detailed and more aware of the complexity of writing as an activity than the average paean to word processors as the ultimate writing tool.
[Composing Processes, Testimonial]

Berul, L. (1973). Natural language text processing. 10th Annual National Information Retrieval Colloquium, Philadelphia, PA. Washington, DC.: American Society for Information Science, 1974, 80-5.

Most of the authors' remarks are focused in the area of full text processing. A few developments in full text retrieval are reviewed and some developments made by the author in the area of computer generated context indexes are discussed.

Billings, K. (1980). Microcomputers and education: Now and in the future. Kilo Baud Microcomputing, 6, 100-2.

The marketing of personal computers, games and word-processing machines has led to interest in introducing computers into the classroom. Word-processing features have made the computer a writing tool as well as one for the tutorial mode. Microcomputers must be used consistently with the teacher's philosophy and the school's curriculum. At present the technology is hindered by lack of appropriate instructional software and lack of information on what can and is being done in education.
[Computer Assisted Instruction]

Birnbaum, I. (1981). Simple PETPRO puts thought into words. Practical Computing, 4(12), 94-6.

PETPRO is a word processing program which runs on the Pet and was designed for school and college use.
[PETPRO]

Bishop, R. L. (1970). Computer analysis of natural language text for style and content in the context of instruction in writing. In Proceedings of a Conference on Computers in the Undergraduate Curricula, The University of Iowa, Iowa City, IA, 1.7-1.11.

> Bishop's program is available for $175 (January 1982) from the Journalism Department, University of Michigan. However, it would probably take some programming to get it to work on a machine other than an Amdhal.
> [Journalism]

Bishop, R. L., et al. (1973). Adapting computer-assisted instruction to the non-programmer. Ann Arbor: University of Michigan. In Resources in Education, January 1974. (ERIC Document Reproduction Service No. ED 081 231)

> Note the date here. JCAI (Journalism Computer-Aided Instruction) allows an instructor to have the computer scan for patterns specified and provides text feedback based on these. The advantage to the program in 1973 was that the instructor did not have to learn a computer language to do so, the entire program being based on "IF. . . THEN" commands, the logic of which was easily grasped by the non-computer expert. A detailed example is provided.
> [Journalism, Computer Aided Instruction]

Bishop, R. L. (1974). Computing in the teaching of journalistic writing skills. On-Line, 3(3), 5-12.
> [Journalism]

Black, J. B., & Moran, T. P. Learning and remembering command names. In Eight short papers in user psychology, Moran, T. P. (editor). Palo Alto, CA: Xerox PARC, 1982, pp. 11-14.

> Important if one is designing word-processing software, but not if one has already bought one. The question is whether the names of commands (e.g., "delete") affect the ease of learning or remembering for novices or experts. Non-computer users describe insert as "add," delete as "omit," replace as "change," and move as "put"; the second list involves higher-frequency English words than does the former, and they are more general and less precise. Alas, it turned out in controlled experiments that the low-frequency, discriminating list was learned faster and remembered longer.
> [Design of Software]

Bleakley, L. A. (1983). The microcomputer and the English department. CSSEDC Quarterly (Conference for Secondary School English Department Chairpersons), 5(2), 7-8.

> A general summary of the kinds of things English teachers do with computers; a call for teacher computer literacy.
> [Computer Literacy]

Block. G. H. (Ed.) (1983). Computers, Reading and Language Arts, 1(1), 62 pp.

The "premier issue" of a journal which promises to provide useful reviews of computer software, in some cases for writing, and a forum of exchanging ideas. Three articles in this issue might be helpful to elementary and secondary writing teachers (Engberg's on word processors in an English classroom, Hasselbring & Owens on spelling analysis, and Suttles' on recent research and innovative programs.)

Booth, A. W., & Baranden, M. S. (1979). Voice input to English text output. International Journal of Man-Machine Studies, 11(6), 681-692.
    [Communication Systems]

Bork, A., & Franklin, S. (1979). Personal computers in learning. Educational Technology, 10, 12.

An introduction to the personal computer as an aid to the learning process. Defines a personal computer as "a general purpose machine conceivably programmable by the user" which "can work primarily alone." Contrasts to a timesharing system, and gives good, clear definitions of hardware and software components. Does not discuss different brands of personal computers. Discusses future prospects, especially in the area of videodisc systems and voice output and (more tentatively) voice input. Some of the things said about microcomputers as tools for educational development are now outdated, due to the increased capabilities of these machines. Provides an overview of CP/M, Mini Unix, and RT-11 (designed for DEC computers only), then argues that UCSD Pascal is the language best suited for educational programming and BASIC is inferior. No mention of writing on a computer at all--the article assumes programming is what you want to do.
    [Design of Software]

Bossone, R. M., & Weiner, M. (1973). Three modes of teaching remedial English: A comparative analysis. City University of New York, New York Bernard Baruch College, CUNY Graduate School and University Center. (ERIC Document Reproduction Service No. ED 074 514)

One mode is computer-aided instruction. This is dated and not very useful.

Bott, R. A. (1979). A study of complex learning: Theory and methodologies (CHIP Report 82), Center for Human Information Processing, University of California at La Jolla.

Bourque, J. H. (1983). Understanding and evaluating: The humanist as computer specialist. College English, 45(1), 67-73.

An interesting dilemma: computer software for writing cannot improve much until humanists get involved with its development, but those who do may not find that their work is valued in their home departments, especially English departments. Bourque suggests six ways such work might be evaluated so that those who pioneer in this field can survive.

Bove, T. (1982) Writing with WORDSTAR: A quick tutorial for beginners. Data Cast 002, 12-42.

A reasonably clear, comprehensive review, but only for someone who has already used another word processor. Does not focus on student writing; the "beginners" are WORDSTAR users, not writers.
[WORDSTAR]

Boynton, G. R. (1982). Computing in universities: Setting up a computerized department. EDUCOM Bulletin, 22-24.

Boynton describes the reasons for supplying each faculty member as well as the clerical staff with a microcomputer networked into the university's main computers. The system is not used to teach students; rather, it is intended to increase the productivity of the faculty and clerical staff. Clear reasons for the choice of hardware and networking software are presented, and the crucial support that will be needed from the computer center staff is emphasized.

Brandt, Ron. (1981). On reading, writing, and computers: A conversation with John Martin Henry. Educational Leadership, 39, 60-64. (ERIC Document Reproduction Service No. EJ 253 758)

Bratley, P., & Lusignan, S. (1978). The electronic scriptorium. Montreal: Univ. de Montreal (Dept. d'informatique Publication #311); published in Computers and the Humanities (1979), 13, 93-104.

An advanced system for automatic analysis, chiefly of literary works. It includes concordances, word-frequency counts, sentence lengths, etc. It is working on Control Data mainframes and IBM. This way of analyzing text structures might be interesting, especially for people who want to do research on student writing.
[Literary Analysis]

Braun, L. (1980) Computers in learning environments: An imperative for the 1980's. BYTE (Computers and Education issue), 5(7), 6-10, 108-114.

Primarily aimed ata elementary and secondary schools, but presents a strong argument for "immediate and dramatic intervention in our educational system in order to take advantage of the many benefits which the computer can contribute." Perhaps the most useful portion of this guest editorial is the annotated list of

persons and organizations who are currently doing just that. Writing and word/text processing does not come up.
[Computer Aided Instruction]

Brenner, G. (1982) Programming and writing: the University of Montana Cooperative Composition Experiment. Paper presented at the College Composition and Communication Convention, San Francisco.

A report of an experiment based on a rather innovative hypothesis: that an interdisciplinary sequence of courses in computer programming, symbolic logic and composition could improve student writing. While the "experiment" is flawed in its design (and Brenner admits this), the problems with the context reported in the paper are as interesting as any results might have been: resistance to computers in English departments, problems with rating essays for quality, etc. Good to read in planning stages so that we can learn from others' errors. Not a bad section comparing learning computer language to learning to write (though elementary).
[Programming]

Brent, E. E., Jr. (1981). Writing with a data-base management system. BYTE, 6(11), 18-34.

Brent claims word processing works best at relatively late stages in the writing process--after recording research results, compiling references, and constructing an outline. This article shows how the database management system, can help in the earlier stages of writing and can be more powerful than a word-processing program for major reorganization of text.
[Data Bases]

Briand, P. L., Jr. (1979). Technology in the teaching of composition. Paper presented at the Conference on College Composition and Communication, Denver, CO. (ERIC Document Reproduction Service No. ED 162 324)

Briand gives a history of technology in the composition classroom, from overhead projectors to computer-assisted instruction. His uses for computers are fairly typical: teaching spelling, grammar, punctuation, and style (using frequency counts of various types of clauses, phrases, verbs, and sentences). The closest he gets to word processing as such is the use of the "electronic character generator," a typewriter which will reproduce characters on a television screen. Briand tends to view this as simply a more powerful audiovisual aid. He mentions a few peoples' work cited here--Robert Bishop, John Riskin. His other uses for the computer are mainly in the form of text feedback. He shares the established view of CAI as a way of freeing the instructor from tedious drilling tasks to concentrate more complex writing problems.
[Computer Aided Instruction, Spelling Drill, Grammar Drill]

Bridwell, L. S., Johnson, P., & Brehe, S. (in press). Composing and computers: Case studies of experienced writers. In Matsuhashi, A., (Ed.), Writing in "Real" Time: Modelling production processes, New York: Longman. Manuscript submitted for publication.

A detailed account to the effects of using computers on eight experienced writers who had not previously used word processing packages. Each of the writers responded to computer composing in different ways, but patterns emerged which have implications for introducing word processing to students.
[Case Study, Composing Processes]

Bridwell, L. S., Nancarrow, P. R., & Ross, D. (1983) The writing process and the writing machine: Current research on word processors relevant to the teaching of composition. In Beach, R, & Bridwell, L. eds., New Directions in composition research. New York: Guilford Press, pp. 381-398.

A critique of much current research and many specific programs useful for writers in college composition classes. Also contains an overview of work in progress in composition classrooms and implications for the future.
[Survey]

Bridwell, L. S., & Ross, D. (in press). Integrating computers into a writing curriculum; or, buying, begging and building. In W. Wresch (Ed.), A writer's tool: The computer in composition instruction. Manuscript submitted for publication.

A summary of the priorities the authors set as they introduced computers into the Composition Program at The University of Minnesota, specifically into junior and senior level courses focusing on writing in one's major field. Reviews the software they chose, including commercially available software, software under development "borrowed" from those designing it, and specifications for software they found they had to develop for themselves.
[Survey, Design of Software]

Bridwell, L. S., Sirc, G., & Brooke, R. (in press). Revising and computing: Case studies of student writers. In S. Freedman (Ed.), The acquisition of written learning: Revision and response. Norwood, NJ: Ablex. Manuscript submitted for publication.

Case studies of five undergraduates in required junior-senior level writing courses, plus results from a survey of three classes which used word processing for composing. Includes detailed accounts of the students' composing processes, e.g., keystroke records of their performance on the computers, revision analyses, and interviews. The students increased their attention to surface level concerns and to formatting with the computer, and claimed that they revised more substantially. The data confirm that three of the five did engage in significantly more sentence and multiple-sentence revision, while all five significantly increased their surface level editing. The survey showed that a majority of the students in computer-assisted classes clearly saw the advantages of using a computer for major revising,

as well as editing.
[Case Study, Composing Processes]

Brillhart, L. V., & Barnett, A. (1980). Humanizing the introduction to computers. AEDS Proceedings of 18th Annual Convention, A Gateway to the use of Computers in Education, St. Louis, MO (Washington, DC), 47–51.

> Discussion concentrates on use of computers by engineering students, but can be applied to all programs. Students who have never used computers are especially in need of a careful introduction to the machines which reduces the anxiety involved in dealing with unfamiliar technology, and minimizes negative feedback.

Brockman, R. J., & McCauley, R. J. (1983). The computer and the writer's craft: Implications for teachers. Paper given at the College Composition and Communication Convention, Detroit and available from the authors at Department of Industrial Technology, Arizona State University, Tempe, AZ.

> Posits a continuum of computer interaction with writing from word processing to "true on line documentation." The former should make no major difference in writing or writing instruction, but it doesn't do much to exploit the full potential of the computer. Radical changes will occur when the computer becomes the medium of communication, where factors other than rhetoric and language must be taken into account. In the middle of the continuum is "integrated software," where word processing, image processing and ordinary computing are available at the same work station, and where a writer is expected to master the whole system (without the help of a secretary, artist, or programmer). On line documentation of computer programs will (or should) take full advantage of the computer, e.g., by having messages controlled by the computer's clock or introducing graphics to illustrate how a mechanism works. As communication moves away from its current paper base, we need to be aware of the effects of the changes.
> [Documentation]

Brown, F. J. (1978). A computer-calculated index. (ERIC Document Reproduction Service No. ED 154 337)

> The Gunning Fog Index was used for essays from a business communication course at Wayne State University to provide variety in the course and warn students when their writing is [allegedly] difficult to read. A procedure for calculating the index by using four computer programs is described and the four programs are listed. Cf. WRITER'S WORKBENCH, and the critique of Gunning in Holland.
> [Readability, WRITER'S WORKBENCH]

Bryan, J. W. (1977). A study of new technology in northern Illinois daily newspapers. Ph.D. dissertation, Northern Illinois University.

Gives brief history of early conversion attempts, describes software available from 1974-77, Rockford Newspapers' conversion. Surveys management by questionnaire. Studies psychological effects in newsroom, composing room.
[Journalism]

Burke, R. L. (1982) CAI sourcebook. Englewood Cliffs, NJ: Prentice Hall.

Discusses computer aided instruction for those who can program and have access to an interactive system. Emphasis is on CAI which involves choosing an answer (choice response) rather than making one up (constructed response), and on simple frame presentations and response processing.
[Computer Aided Instruction, Survey]

Burns, H. L. (1979) Stimulating invention in English composition through computer-assisted instruction. Unpublished doctoral dissertation, University of Texas at Austin.

Describes a study of a computer-assisted invention program used in four freshman composition classes which employed questions drawn from Aristotle's enthymeme topics, Kenneth Burke's dramatistic pentad, and the Young-Becker-Pike tagmemic matrix. (The original package was called INVENT, and included three programs: TOPOI, BURKE, and TAGI.) The study found that invention CAI can encourage growth in the amount and complexity of ideas a student produces, that "dialogues" with a computer can help students formulate and develop their ideas as well as retain them, even though the computer can't actually deal with the content of those ideas, and that open-ended CAI designed to foster creativity by widening a student's perspective on a subject is programmable.
[INVENT]

Burns, H. (1980). Education's new management: The personal computing underground. Pipeline 20, 41.

Speculation on what the effects of students' personal computers might be on their study habits and techniques; implications for teachers. Mentions word processors briefly. General.

Burns, H. (1981). Computing as a way of brainstorming in English composition. In Harris, D., (ed.), Proceedings of the National Educational Computing Conference (NECC) (pp. 105-108). The University of Iowa, Iowa City, IA.

Burns, H. (1981). Pandora's chip: Concerns about quality CAI. Pipeline, 15-16, 49.

Very general assessment of CAI with brief reference to Burns's work on invention strategies.
[Computer Aided Instruction, INVENT]

Burns, H. (1981). A writer's tool: Computing as a mode of inventing. Paper presented at the New York College English Association Conference (Saratoga Springs, N.Y.). (ERIC Document Reproduction Service No. ED 193 693)

See also Burns's dissertation. Burns maintains that invention programs are a viable alternative to the typical drill and practice sequences which so much English CAI is devoted to, and that the interactive nature of the computer can help students explore a subject area by dredging up half-formed ideas, by making students write them down and clarify them, and by asking questions which might not occur to the student and for which the student might not have answers. The computer session thus generates some dissonance and helps uncover problems worth exploring in a paper. Burns emphasizes the value of such a program as a "conference tool," since it can provide much more time (approximately 560 conference hours) for learning the techniques of invention than can the average instructor. Students can also get printouts of their interaction with the computer.
[Computer Aided Instruction, INVENT]

Burns, H. (1983). Computer-assisted prewriting activities: Harmonics for invention. In R. W. Lawler, Computers in composition instruction. Los Alamitos, CA: SWRL Educational Research and Development.

This paper is well written and a good introduction to Burns's work. The explanation given as to why a computer is being used in this writing task is well thought out and useful in providing guidelines for others. His distinction between invention as a "solo" (student alone) as opposed to a "duet" (student prompted and encouraged by teacher) leads finally to a discussion of "electronic orchestration" of such activity via the computer. A lengthy example of a student using Burn's programs to generate material for a senior literature seminar paper is provided.
[INVENT]

Burns, H., & Culp, G. (1980). Stimulating invention in English composition through computer-assisted instruction. Educational Technology, 20, 5-10.

Burns is one of the few people who have designed CAI for composition with an emphasis on helping students with the early stages of the writing process. A more descriptive summary of the same research is given in the annotation for Burns's dissertation.

Burns, R. E., Davisson, W. I., & Kline, E. A. (no date) CAI and the microprocessor. Unpublished manuscript. Department of English, The University of Notre Dame, South Bend, IN.
[Computer Aided Instruction]

One of several papers available from Notre Dame on their work to incorporate CAI into their composition program. Programs available fall into five categories: morphology, syntax, punctuation, spelling, and phonology. They are used to

support traditional writing classes; definite "remedial" focus. This paper illustrates the uses of CAI for spelling problems and discusses programming concerns (using BASIC, something they've developed called CAI Author Language, running on TRS/80's.)
[Remedial, Spelling Drill, Grammar Drill]

Burns, R. E., Davisson, W. I., & Kline, E. A. (no date). Computer–managed tutorials at Notre Dame. Unpublished manuscript, available from English Department, University of Notre Dame, South Bend, IN.

A paper available from Notre Dame describing their university–wide uses of CAI. They report high levels of student satisfaction with this form of remedial instruction. English lessons are exclusively grammar and spelling, some 57 of them. Basic question–answer–response mode of CAI. Widely disseminated program (they mention exporting materials to 22 other institutions).
[Computer Aided Instruction, Grammar Drill, Spelling Drill]

Burton, R., Brown, R., & Seely, J. (1978). Intelligent CAI: An author aid for a natural language interface. Washington: Advanced Research Projects Agency (DOD). In O'Neill, H. F. (Ed.), (1979). Instructional System Development. New York: Academic Press. (ERIC Document Reproduction Service No. ED 165 797)

Addresses the problems of using natural language (English) as the communication language for advanced computer–based instructional systems, usually problem solving in engineering or mathematics. Quite technical, and of use only to people really interested in computers and natural language. Considers issues such as the efficiency, tutorial capability, and tolerance of ambiguity, especially pronominalizations and ellipses, required by a natural language understanding system, and discusses the implementation of a semantic grammar on the SOPHIE system, first using LISP grammar, then an Augmented Transition Network.
[Syntax]

Byerly, G. (1978). Generating English programs at a small college. In Prather, R. E. (Ed.), Proceedings of the 1978 Conference on Computers in the Undergraduate Curricula. University of Denver, Denver, CO.

Byerly, G. A. (1978). CAI in college English. Computers and the Humanities, 12, 281–285.

A good review article––it treats at some length PLATO, developed by Control Data, TICCIT, from Brigham Young University, Susan Wittig's programs developed at the University of Texas at Austin, Edward Kline's grammar programs (Notre Dame), IBM's COMSKL, designed for remedial instruction, Vivian Rudisill's Multimedia English Laboratory at San Antonio, and PRESS, part of a poetry analysis program created by Andries van Dam at Brown University.

[PLATO, Grammar Drill, Literary Analysis, Computer Aided Instruction]

Cakir, A. D., Hart, J., & Stewart, T. F. M. (1979) Visual Display Terminals. The Inca-Fieej Research Association, Darmstadt. Also published in 1980 by John Wiley & Sons, New York.

[Survey of Hardware]

Caldwell, R. (1979). Guidelines for developing basic skills instructional materials for use with microcomputer technology. Educational Technology, 20.

Beginning level how-to for those interested in developing CAI programs for surface level problems in writing.

[Computer Aided Instruction]

Caldwell, R. (1980). The acquisition of language skills using computer-based instruction. In Purves, Alan (Ed.), Cognition and written language: A symposium. (ERIC Document Reproduction Service No. ED 178 918)

Outlines the advantages of CAI for language skills; does not discuss word processors. The paper's purpose is "to discuss the salient attributes of a 'meaningful language experience' and to describe means to achieve such an experience regardless of a learner's socioeconomic background." Caldwell sees computer-based instruction as the solution to inequalities in verbal learning environments because of its ability to provide individualized, graded instruction so that educationally disadvantaged students can "catch up": a rather ironic solution considering that schools in low-income areas have difficulty obtaiaining access to the kind of technology Caldwell proposes so they can "change the balance" for their students.

[Computer Aided Instruction]

Camelot: A microcomputer-based instructional system. (1982). Paper available from Miami-Dade Community College, Miami, FL.

A description of a "stand-alone computer environment" for individualized instruction (similar to RSVP; see Anandam or Kotler) except that its goal is greater portability with many participating institutions. Its four subsystems include GUINIVERE (a user-checking system which matches programs to users); ARTHUR (an interactive program for faculty to set up their own programs); LANCELOT ("the Doer," initiates and maintains a friendly dialogue with faculty as they enter student information, score tests, print feedback for students, and prepare final class reports); and MERLYN (an interactive subsystem for giving faculty information on instructional design and use of the systems). Not specifically for writing, but writing feedback is one of the things it can be used for.

[RSVP]

Canter, D., & Davis, I. (1982). Ergonomic parameters of word processors in use. Displays, Technology & Applications, 3(2), 81–8.

> Discusses results of questionnaire completed by 342 respondents, and interviews within 26 organizations, about the design and use of word current processors. The ancillary features bothered people: the design and use of their desks/chairs, the lack of storage space, printer noise, etc. Most word processor users are new to their machines and have limited applications for them; they rarely have experience with other machines.
> [Human Factors]

Card, C. (1979). Standardizing languages for word and text processing. CIPS (Canadian Information Processing Society) Review, 3(2), 26–27.

> Describes the background and status of a project begun under the direction of the American National Standards Institute to standardize computer languages for text processing.
> [Design of Software]

Card, S. K. (1978). Studies in the psychology of computer text editing systems. Xerox Palo Alto Research Center [SSL-78-1], Palo Alto, CA. Unpublished manuscript.

> This was Card's dissertation. The focus is on comparing various systems on various computers. Editing is actually transcribing marks from an annotated manuscript into the system to see how fast it gets done. Card does not explore how or why those marks got there, nor is the person who runs the system responsible for any changes in language.
>
> All computer editors were faster than typing, both for running text and for changing things. Hard copy editors take more time than screen editors. An editor's speed (for these tasks) is a function of the number of keystrokes. It's more efficient to type slowly but make fewer mistakes than to type fast and make more errors.
>
> See Ch. 8, pp. 187–190 for a discussion of cognitive processes (and memory) involved in editing, and the difference between editing and problem solving.
> [Case Study, Human Factors, Design of Software]

Card, S. K. (1979). A method for calculating performance times for users of interactive computer systems. Report from International Conference on Cybernetics and Society, 653–658. Institute of Electrical and Electronics Engineers, New York.

> Addresses the issue of which might be the best way to program a word processor, to do a specific task, for example, backspacing to delete a word. Interesting for those who are designing systems, but too precise for those who are merely amateurs using them.
> [Design of Software]

Card, S. (1982). User perception mechanisms in the search of computer command menus. In T. P. Moran (Ed.), Eight short papers in user psychology. Palo Alto, CA: Xerox PARC, pp. 225–31.

Discussion for system designers of how people find what they want on a menu. The first search is faster for an alphabetic menu, than for a functionally arranged one; both are much faster than a randomly arranged menu. The practiced user finds any arrangement the same. Perceptually, items are chunked between one item and the one below it, or, if boxes are used, within the box.
[Human Factors]

Card, S. K. (in press). Visual search of computer command menus. Bouma, H. and Bouwhuis, D. (Eds.), Attention and Performance X. Hillsdale, NJ: Lawrence Erlbaum Associates.

Technical report: interesting for people who design on-screen menus. Searches seem to be unsystematic until users get oriented to the particular menu (no matter how the menu was organized).
[Design of Software]

Card, S. K., English, W. K., & Burr, B. J. (1978). Evaluation of mouse, rate-controlled isometric joystick, step keys, and text keys for text selection on a CRT. Ergonomics, 21, 601–613.

Mouse, joystick, step keys, and text keys are hardware gadgets which move the cursor.
[Design of Hardware]

Card, S. K., Moran, T. P, & Newell, A. (1976) The manuscript editing task: a routine cognitive skill. Palo Alto, CA. Xerox Palo Alto Research Center [SSL-76-8], December 1976, 77 pp.

Correcting a marked-up manuscript. Elaborations of cognitive-psychology models of how the behavior should be described. The experimental process, especially the hardware (videotape, etc.) and some definitions of behavior at the keyboard may be useful for designing future experiments. The error analysis typing looks good.
[Design of Hardware]

Card, S. K., Moran. T. P., & Newell, A. (1980). Computer text-editing: An information-processing analysis of a routine cognitive skill. Cognitive Psychology, 12(1), 32–74.

An information-processing model that describes how a person uses an interactive computer text-editing system to modify a manuscript. The behavior of an expert user can be modeled by giving his goals, operators, methods, and selection rules for choosing among alternatives. The paper assesses such a model with respect to

(1) predicting user behavior sequences, (2) predicting the time required to do particular modifications, and (3) determining the effect on accuracy of the detail with which the modelling is done (the model's 'grain size'). Timed task protocols from several users are examined. Users' choices (involving, for example, leaving "insert" off and reformatting, or vice versa) are predicted about 80% of the time by a few simple manuscript-editing tasks.
[Design of Software, Human Factors]

Card, S. K., Moran, T. P., & Newell, A. (1980) The keystroke level-model for user performance time with interactive systems. Communications of the ACM, 23(7), 396-410.

Aside from potential uses in designing experiments, outlined in the annotation of the report above, this article (and others by Card, et al.) may have implications for the strategies instructors recommend to students for writing on a word processor--for example, what's the best way to move a block of text? how does that change when the student becomes an expert? etc. Article primarily deals with a model for measuring the amount of time an expert user takes to perform a given task on a computer system, so that systems may be designed more efficiently and ergonomically. See also Card (1979).
[Human Factors, Case Study]

Caro, R. (1980). How to approach selecting the right word processor. Modern Office and Data Management, 19(3), 21-2.

As the periodical's name suggests, this is oriented around office needs, so it discusses how paperwork an office produces relates to the choice of a word processor. It also discusses such things as keyboard layout, text moving, and storage capacity.
[Survey of Hardware]

Carrigan, B. (1980). Automated text editing. Unpublished manuscript.

Bibliography of federally-funded research; contains 232 citations from the National Technical Information Service, Springfield, VA data base on automatic text editing and composing. Discusses programming techniques for processing lists, and for report, index, and table generation.
[Bibliography]

Cary, C. D. (1979). A user's view of WORDS. Computers and the Humanities, 13(2), 129-130.

Cason, W. C. (1982). Menu manager. IBM Technical Disclosure Bulletin, 24(8), 4125-6.

Describes a general purpose software utility program for controlling menus.

[Design of Software]

Catano, J. V. (1979).   Poetry and computers: Experimenting with a communal text.
Computers and the Humanities, 13(4), 269–275.

Discusses HYPERTEXT, a program for sharing analysis of literary texts, developed
at Brown University under Robert Scholes' direction.
[Literary Analysis]

Cavin, C. S., Cavin, E. D., & Culp, G. (1980).   A survey on computer assisted
instruction at the University of Texas at Austin.   SIGCUE Bulletin, 14(2), 13–17.

Reports on a questionnaire administered to the faculty of the University of Texas
at Austin in the spring of 1978, to see whether respondents thought CAI should
be used more or less, and what the significant problems were for development of
new CAI and expansion of faculty use.   Those who used CAI were asked
questions about what they were using and where it came from, the need for
background in computers and programming to use and/or develop CAI, and the
degree of background the programmer or developer should have in the subject
matter.
[Computer Aided Instruction, Survey of Software]

Cecil, P. B. (1980).   Word processing in the modern office.   2nd
ed. Benjamin/Cummings Publishing.
[Office of Future]

Celko, J. (1982).   Computer fixes spelling faster than a scrawl.   Infosystems, April 5,
1982, 34–6.
[Spelling Checkers]

Chamberlin, D. D., et al. (1981).   Janus: An interactive system for document
composition.   Proceedings of the ACM SIGPLAN/SIGOA Symposium on Text
Manipulation.

On typesetting, not on writing or editing.
[Typesetting]

Cherry, L. L. (1980).   PARTS--a system for assigning word classes to English text.
(Computing Science Technical Report No. 81.) Bell Laboratories, Murray Hill, NJ.

The program assigns parts of speech at 340 words per second, at 95% accuracy.
As noted in Cherry's "Computer Aids for Writers," it is embedded in Bell Lab's
WRITER'S WORKBENCH (which operates on UNIX).   A modest dictionary of
400 words (mostly function words and irregular verbs) is found first, then a list

of suffixes (Latinate) gets some nouns and content words. Finally, a "scan" program looks for verbs and nouns.

Technical comment: The description doesn't mention a separate procedure for finding and isolating prepositional phrases, after the model of EYEBALL.   If it isn't there, it probably should be.   This does illustrate the advantage of having a verb dictionary in a parser.   As a parsing grammar, it would become (linguistically) more powerful if it included grammatical function, along the lines of Dirk Geens' work on automatic parsing and EYEBALL.
[EYEBALL, WRITER'S WORKBENCH]

Cherry, L. (1981).   Computer aids for writers.   <u>Proceedings of the ACM SIGPLAN</u>, <u>16</u>(6), 61-67.

In addition to briefer descriptions of the STYLE and DICTION programs, this article also surveys other systems developed by Bell Laboratories, most of which have been incorporated into The WRITER'S WORKBENCH.   PARTS, whose purpose is to assign word classes (by means of "tokens" rather than "types"), makes STYLE, PROSE, REWRITE, TOPIC, and SPLITINF possible.   PROSE uses some of STYLE's statistics to compare the text under examination to standards calculated from "good" examples of the same type of document; so far only technical papers and training documents have such standards calculated for them. REWRITE, based on R. A. Lanham's <u>Revising Prose</u>, locates prepositions, to be verbs, and empty phrases (using DICTION), and highlights them by capitalization. TOPIC is intended to provide key words or index entries; it locates frequent noun phrases in the text.   This has possibilities for rush writing, since it's very similar to "looping" through a rush write for ideas or feelings which come up repeatedly: can it be modified to locate verbs and adjectives as well? The program might also be used as a revising tool to find overused words.   The last program based on PARTS, SPLITINF, locates split infinitives.   Cherry describes three other copy editing programs: SPELL (a dictionary spelling checker), DOUBLE (which looks for words twice in succession, a common error in computer-edited text), and PUNCT, which checks for unbalanced quotes or parentheses, fixes spaces around dashes, etc.

The authors of each program are listed in the acknowledgments: W. Vesterman consulted with Cherry for STYLE and DICTION; M. D. MacIlroy wrote SPELL; N. H. Macdonald is responsible for PROSE, SPLITINF, DOUBLE, and PUNCT.
[Spelling Checkers, WRITER'S WORKBENCH]

Cherry, L. L. (1982).   Writing tools.   <u>IEEE Transactions on Professional Communication</u> (Special Issue on Communications in the Automated Office), <u>30</u>(1), 100-105.

See Cherry and Vesterman, below.
[WRITER'S WORKBENCH]

Cherry, L. L., & Vesterman, W. (1980). Writing tools—the STYLE and DICTION programs. Murray Hill, NJ: Bell Laboratories Technical Report; (1981). Computational Linguistics.

Designed primarily for business and/or technical writers. STYLE analyzes text using readability formulas (Kincaid, automated, Coleman–Liau, and Flesch), computing statistics for average sentence and word length, as well as for "nonfunction" words (nouns, adjectives, adverbs, and non-auxiliary verbs), which may be used to compare differences in word choice among writers more accurately than a word count including prepositions, conjunctions, articles, and auxiliary verbs. STYLE also indicates the percentage of short and long sentences, whether they are simple, complex, compound, and/or compound–complex, and how many begin with what Cherry terms "subject openers": nouns, pronouns, possessives, adjectives, or articles. (Sentences so counted may not really reflect the number of sentences which open with their subject, but Cherry asserts that the category is still useful for pointing out a lack of variety in sentence openers). The program also reveals how often various parts of speech appear in the text as a whole.

DICTION prints out sentences containing frequently misused or verbose phrases. The user may create her own file, which allows her to include words she wishes to keep tabs on, as well as to suppress, patterns found in the default file. She may run the program with both patterns files or just one. DICTION also works in conjunction with a program called SUGGEST, an interactive thesaurus providing alternative phrases for those DICTION has listed as possible problems. SUGGEST works word by word, as prompted by the user.

STYLE has definite limitations in terms of grammatical accuracy and scope: the inability to distinguish sentence fragments and run–ons being the most crucial. DICTION makes no attempt to group similar errors in usage together, to explain errors, or to distinguish between different types or degrees of "bad" usage. Cherry claims these programs "may be applied to documents on any subject with equal accuracy," (p. 11), but examples are drawn largely from technical documents. The programs provide useful information which can teach intermediate writers much about their personal writing styles, but they are not designed primarily as pedagogical tools, nor are they designed for beginning writers.
[Readability, WRITER'S WORKBENCH]

Coburn, P., et al. (1982). Practical guide to computers in education. Reading, MA: Addison, Wesley.

Coffey, M. (1982). The better bulletin board system. Creative Computing 8(12), 20–26.

Describes a program, "Communitree," written for the Apple II or II+, which should allow for electronic mail to be exchanged. The system lets one follow a whole series of messages. Coffey finds the commands easy for naive users to master, so this program may work to simulate conference groups or teacher-

student interchanges.
[Communications Systems]

Cohen. J. D. (1976). The text justifier TJ6. MIT Artificial Intelligence Memo #358.

Note the date. The memo is a reference and user's manual. The program "can justify and fill text; automatically number pages and figures; control page format and indentation; underline, superscript and subscript; print a table of contents; etc."
[Typesetting]

Cohen, M. E. (1981). HOMER information sheet. Unpublished manuscript. Available from Michael E. Cohen, UCLA Writing Programs. UCLA Los Angeles, CA 90024.

A text feedback program based, like parts of WRITER'S WORKBENCH, on Richard Lanham's textbook advice on composing, but unlike WRITER'S WORKBENCH, this is tailored specifically for students. According to this information sheet, HOMER is soon to be incorporated into a "teaching" word processor (the WANDAH system Cohen and Ruth Von Blum are currently working on). The program has some interesting features, including "verbal maps" of one's composition based on parts of speech used and sentence length, which are helpful visual aids that allow the student to see skeletal structures, mini lessons on usage, and text printed with targeted words isolated in the left margin. HOMER has a sense of humor that may be a bit too sarcastic for the tender-hearted freshman; its (his?) irony would at times be unclear to a novice student writer. But the HOMER program makes it quite clear to students that the computer is only a machine scanning verbal surfaces, not a genuine reader; that's important. A clear sample run of the program is provided.
[HOMER, WANDAH]

Coke, E. U. (1982). Computer aids for writing text. In Jonassen, D. H., (Ed.), The Technology of Text. Educational Technology Publishers.

Cole, B. C. (1981). Computer networking in education. Interface Age. 6(10), 88–93.

Describes how teachers and educators everywhere have worked, in tight financial times, to put together low cost personal computer networks, ranging from sharing of disks and printers to large university networks of personal computers, to even larger local networks, all the way up to complex configurations resembling Ethernet.
[Communication Systems]

Collier, R. M. (1982). The influence of computer-based text editors on the revision strategies of inexperienced writers. Paper presented at the Northwest Regional Conference on the Teaching of English in the Two-year college, 26 pp. Available from the author, Mount Royal College, Calgary, Alberta, Canada.

Preliminary attempt to assess differences for inexperienced writers between handwritten methods of revision and revision performed on a word processor/text editor. Four first-year students used the AES terminals at Mount Royal College in Calgary, Alberta for six weeks. The actual nature of the revising strategies did not change; only the number of revisional alterations and the speed at which these alterations were made changed significantly. However, subjects revised more willingly and enthusiastically, Collier reports, when using the word processor than when revising in the traditional mode. But the AES equipment was simply too complex and cumbersome: the need to shift attention from content to word processing mechanics was distracting. He concludes that the more experienced subjects become with the terminals, the more effective, as well as efficient, their revision strategies become; but, to his knowledge, word processing terminals have not yet been built sufficiently "user-friendly" for direct application in the writing lab. When word processors are designed with split screens, review programs, and simplified command sequences, Collier maintains, they will become an integral part of the writing lab. Recent work developing micro-based word processors for student and teacher use (e.g., Cohen, Von Blum) is going in that direction. Collier suggests that while the use of a word processor for revision is a definite advantage for already capable writers and doesn't hurt the average writer, the word processor simply makes more efficient the deep habits and revision paradigms which the subject already has and uses; this study, however, seems too preliminary and confined for such a suggestion to be conclusive.
[Case Study]

Collier, R. M. (1983). The word processor and revision strategies. College Composition and Communication, 34, 149-155.

Presents results discussed in the annotation of his earlier paper (1982). Concludes that two things must happen to make computers really useful in college classes: 1) Students will have to become sufficiently "computer literate" to make composing and revising on a word processor a practical alternative to writing by hand; 2) Our electronic engineers will have to redesign the word processor so that it demonstrably supports and enhances the writing process.
[Case Study]

Collins, A. (no date) Teaching reading and writing with personal computers. Bolt Beranek and Newman Inc., Cambridge, MA 02238.

Collins' article is primarily a survey of existing computer-assisted reading and writing activities, focussed on young children. Besides a handy compendium, Collins offers a rationale for why computers are ideally suited to the inculcation of these skills due to their generative and interactive capabilities (e.g., a program like STORY MAKER, discussed in Rubin and Zaccher, below) as well as their creation of an environment in which the products children create (writing) or the skills they need to learn (reading) are based on children communicating with other

children.
[STORY MAKER]

Collins, A., Bruce, B. & Rubin, A. (1982). Microcomputer-based writing activities for the upper elementary grades. In Proceedings of the Fourth International Learning Technology Congress and Exposition. Warrenton, VA: Society for Applied Technology.

> Basically, a plan for a curriculum formed around the memory and editing abilities of the Apple II. The authors envision creating a "Library" and "Message Center" with the computer, which students can use to store, retrieve, and share information with other classes. Each class will form "clubs" and "projects" whose work will be stored in the computer, and responded to by the appropriate "clubs" in other classes via computer. Their system will require: (1) a children's text editor; (2) a publication system; (3) a message system; (4) an information storage system; (5) an activities-creating system.
> [STORY MAKER]

Collins, A., & Gentner, D. (1980). A framework for a cognitive theory of writing. In Gregg, L. W., & Steinberg, E. R. (Eds.), Cognitive processes in writing. Hillsdale, NJ: Lawrence Erlbaum Associates, Publishers.

> A theoretical discussion of the relationship between emerging cognitive process models of writing and the computer's power to produce polished texts, teach, and provide insights into composing processes. They envision a "computer-based 'Writing Land'" and offer their speculations about how computers could apply composing process theory to both idea generation and text production.
> [Composing Processes]

Collins, A., & Rubin, A. (1980). How the cognitive sciences will impact education. Unpublished manuscript, available from the authors, c/o Bolt Beranek and Newman, Cambridge, MA 02238

> Discusses StoryMaker in elementary classes as an illustration of the theory that microcomputers can teach novices about higher-level structures while the micros handle troublesome lower-level structures. Suggestive, and well based in cognitive theory.
> [STORY MAKER]

Colson, J. (1975). Contribution to the description of style. Folia Linguistica, 7(3-4), 339-356.

Comer, D., & Shen, V. Y. (1982). Hash-bucket search: A fast technique for searching an English spelling dictionary. Software--Practice & Experience, 12(7), 669-682.
> [Spelling Checkers]

Reviews and compares methods for computer checking with an English spelling dictionary, and presents hash-bucket search, a new technique for dictionary searching. Advantages over existing methods and a sample run are presented.

Conkling, R. D. (1983).   The nuts and bolts of selecting a computer assisted instructional program. T. H. E. Journal, 10(6),

Overview of criteria in the face of combined confusion and enthusiasm. Conkling is (properly) concerned about the purchase of equipment before its potential use is understood, and he gives a helpful checklist which covers the location of hardware and storage of software, training of staff, student access time, and the like.
[Survey of Hardware]

Courtier, G. (1981). Word machines for word people. Publisher's Weekly, February 13, 1981, 219, 40-3.

Cousins, N. (1966).   The computer and the poet. Saturday Review, July 23, 1966.
[Testimonial]

Covey, M. J., & Southwell, M. G. (1983).   Using computers in teaching reasoning and writing. Collegiate Microcomputer, 1, 141-145.

A brief note reporting on a 1983 conference at Carnegie-Mellon. Mainly useful for a catalogue of some of the projects underway around the country and programs being developed and tested, e.g., DRAFT (Christine Neuwirth, Carnegie-Mellon), The COMP-LAB Writing Modules (Michael Southwell, York College, NY), and ANALYTIC (Preston Covey and Bill Chismar, Carnegie-Mellon). Participants stressed that computers can be used to teach formal logic and problem-solving in writing.
[Composing Processes]

Cox, A. E. (1978).   Taking off the blindfolds. Word Processing Now (Great Britain), November, 8, 11.

Examines the capabilities of screen-based word processing, and offers suggestions on how to determine their usefulness for specific needs.
[Testimonial]

Critchfield, M. (1979).   Beyond CAI: Computers as personal intellectual tools. Educational Technology, 19(10), 18-25.

An excellent article for anyone who thinks of computers solely in terms of traditional CAI. Though it only briefly mentions text editing, the approach towards computers as "convivial" rather than "manipulative" technology (the author

is quoting Ivan Illich) produces a focus on learning with computers which is a refreshing corrective to limited drill and practice. Critchfield discusses three kinds of computer learning, in the form of "computer experience": computer experience as a medium for scientific experiment and problem solving simulations, computer experience as a medium for artistic creation (writing is unfortunately not considered here), and computer experience as a medium for acquiring information.
[Computer Aided Instruction]

Croft, M. (1983). Theresa joins the staff: A microcomputer in the writing lab. Unpublished paper presented at the Writing Centers Association Fifth Annual Conference, Purdue University. Available from the author, University of Wisconsin at Stevens Point.

Cronnell, B. (1982). Computer instruction for generating and revising/editing narrative text. Southwest Regional Laboratory Working Paper (2-82/02), available from SWRL, 4665 Lampson Ave., Los Alamitos, CA 90720.

Proposal for a system to follow a screening of a picture story with questions that help the student write his or her own narrative. Correction and stylistic routines are also projected. No references to other story-writer programs for primary grades.
[Computer Aided Instruction]

Cronnell, B. (1982). Computer-based practice in editing. Southwest Regional Laboratory Working Paper (2-82/04), available from SWRL, 4665 Lampson Ave., Los Alamitos, CA 90720.

Proposal for a system to help students review mechanics through practice, and to receive and monitor the students' typing from dictation. No citations of earlier, similar projects.
[Grammar Drill]

Cronnell, B. (1982). Computer instruction for generating and revising/editing narrative text. Working Paper 2-82/02; available from SWRL Educational Research and Development, 4665 Lampson Avenue, Los Alamitos, CA 90720.

Cronnell, B., and Humes, A. (1981). Using microcomputers for composition instruction. Unpublished paper, available from SWRL Educational Research and Development, 4665 Lampson Avenue, Los Alamitos, CA 90720. (ERIC Document Reproduction Service No. ED 203 872)

Elementary and secondary school orientation, but applicable to college writing. Discusses word processors as a writing tool and an improvement over pen and paper; the assumption underlying their enthusiasm is one most of us hope is true

but as yet have no solid evidence for: that since revision is easier on a word processor, students will do more of it. The article claims to focus on the potential for composing on a word processor, but in fact treats revising and editing concerns more than drafting: word processors would be helpful for exercises in revising prewritten text, organizing sentences into paragraphs, sentence combining, checking for errors of spelling and usage. Invention prompts are also brought up as a "possibility," as well as doing descriptive writing on a computer which "draws" what you're describing as you write. Most of these "potential" activities are already being implemented, so the speculative quality of this piece is somewhat misleading; these are not ideas the authors think "might be nice," but ideas that are being developed.
[Spelling Checkers, Invention]

Cronnell, B., & Humes, A. (1982). Computers, word processors, and composition instruction. WCRA Journal, 2(1), 1-2.

Daigon, A. (1966). Computer grading of English composition. English Journal, 55, 46-52.

The system checks spelling against a dictionary of "1000 misspellings which account for over 90 per cent of spelling errors." It also criticizes usage by comparison with a dictionary of common "violations" like "don't hardly," and "real good." It criticizes punctuation in certain contexts (e.g., checks for the comma following sentence-initial "yes" or "no"). It criticizes style on the basis of syntax and other factors--for example, the presence of subordinate conjunctions, relative pronouns, common prepositions, and vocabulary richness (by comparison with the Dale list of 1000 common words).
[Evaluation of Writing, Spelling Checkers]

Daiute, C. (1981). Child-appropriate text editing. Paper presented at the Conference on Child-appropriate Computing, New York City.
[Design of Software]

Daiute, C. (1982). Children and adults write notes to the computer. In Parents League Review 138-144.

A well-written and enjoyable article, worth reading for anyone interested in how children and adults differ in their response to learning text editors. Adults, Daiute notes, have more resistance to and difficulty with using the computer for writing, partly because of ingrained fears, and partly because their memories work differently: adults find it necessary to know why commands work the way they do, to fit individual pieces of information into already existing theories about how computers work or might work. She discusses, fruitfully, differences in anxiety level, ability to master commands, the amounts of assistance needed for adults as opposed to for children (adults generally need more, in spite of the fact that they buy manuals and take copious notes at demonstrations), requests for information, and other general concerns. The adults Daiute worked with were mostly professionals in language areas, the children elementary school level. It's hard to say precisely what the implications are for college level students, most of whom have often had more exposure to computers, outside of writing situations, than had these adults, but the range of different styles of learning computer commands is itself worth knowing about—on a smaller scale, it will no doubt be replicated in any classroom situation where students have varying degrees of resistance to computers.

[Composing Processes, Elementary Writing]

Daiute, C. (1982). Where has all the paper gone? Electronic Learning, Jan. 1982.

Daiute, C. (1982). Word processing: Can it make even good writers better? Electronic Learning, March/April, 1982, 29–31.

A brief article which asks a question we wish we could answer, but, unfortunately she is only asking the question. Useful as a very general introduction to word processing for teachers. Has a good chart which includes most of the widely used systems for word processing, their costs, and the hardware they run on.

Daiute, C. (1983). The computer as stylus and audience. College Composition and Communication, 34, 134–145.

Explores the notions that a word processing system can overcome psychological barriers such as limits to short-term memory and the difficulty of taking the readers' point of view. She also focuses on how the system bypasses the slow physical process of recopying the text.

The difficulty of imagining (or simulating) a reader can be overcome through computer-based "dialogue," especially on-screen prompting statements. The main elements of computer programs which could help are 1) typing is faster than handwriting, especially when retyping is not needed, 2) ordinary text-editor commands are "hotter" than a typewriter or paper and pencil, 3) electronic mail situations could enhance the impression that writing has an audience, 4) feedback programs focus on mistakes. Daiute ends with assertions that computer-based writers, especially children, have no trouble knowing that they control the computer.

[Composing Processes]

Daiute, C. (in press). Computers and writing. New York: Addison-Wesley Publishing Co.

A good introduction to the ways writers—from elementary school children to technical writers in business and industry—can use computers for composing. The

writer discusses the strengths and weaknesses of word processing technology for the whole range of writers.
[Composing Processes]

Daiute, C., O'Brien, P., Shield, A., Liff, S., Wright, P., Mazur, S., & Jawitc, W. (1983). The computer in the writing class: Problems and potentials. Proceedings of NECC/5, National Educational Computing Conference 1983 (Silver Spring, MD: Institute of Electrical and Electronics Engineers Computer Society Press), 22-26.

Guidelines for introducing word processors, with special emphasis on their value to aid revision. Student examples, teachers' reactions are quoted at length. The preliminary results are that children like the technology, but the better typists like it more. Inexperienced users prefer a word processor with few but less abstract and less powerful commands. Revising at the computer seems to stimulate more extensive revising on paper. The computer may be especially helpful with less skilled writers who have a negative view of their writing.
[Composing Processes]

Daiute, C., & Taylor, R. (1981). Computers and improvement of writing. Paper delivered at the Association of Computing Machinery Conference. Reprints are available from the author, Harvard University.

Introductory discussion on composition research, with special emphasis on how writing requires one to "hold a large number of different types of information in short-term memory." The text editor can help alleviate some of the problems. The authors recommend dividing word processor commands into those most useful for composing (e.g., insert, save), those for editing (insert, copy), and those for printing, and introducing students to one group at a time. Daiute and Taylor conclude with typical claims--composing and revising are easier, thus more effective and more extensive--those claims are to be tested empirically.
[Composing Processes]

Damren, N. S. (1980). Smart technical writer picks dumb terminal. Computerworld, March 31, 1980.
[Testimonial]

Davies, D. J. (1982). String searching in text editors. Software--Practice and Experience, 12, 709-17.

Gives data on string lengths and text scanned in routine searching to help people design efficient algorithms.
[Search for Strings, Design of Software]

Davies, D. W., & Yates, D. M. (1978). Human factors in display terminal procedures. Proceedings of the Fourth International Conference on Computer Communication (pp.

777-783). International Council for Computer Communication.
[Human Factors]

Davis, J. E., & Davis, H. K. (Eds.) (1983). Computers in Language Arts [Special Issue]. FOCUS: Teaching English Language Arts, 9(3).

> A special issue of this journal published by the Southeastern Ohio Council of Teachers of English and the Ohio University Department of English Language and Literature. Contains 26 articles which should be useful for beginners and those planning computer-assisted writing courses. See specific annotations of articles by Appleby, Hunter, and Marling.

de Beaugrande, R. (1979). Theoretical foundations of the automatic production and processing of technical reports. Journal of Technical Writing and Communication, 9(3).

> Technical. Discusses the issues and approaches for designing a computer system capable of reading, understanding, and writing technical reports, using advances in computer science and artificial intelligence research to describe how such a system would be configured. A sample text on the origins of sunspots is used as a hypothetical example for how such reading and writing would work. The author makes some procedural suggestions for approaching the problem of correlating syntax and semantics in English. Structural diagrams are provided.
> [Semantics]

Della-Piana, G. M. (1971). The development of a model for the systematic teaching of the writing of poetry. Final Report (BR-O-H-004), University of Utah, Bureau of Educational Research and Development (DHEW/OE). (ERIC Document Reproduction Service No. ED 101 359)

> Describes an early project to develop a program for teaching poetry writing and the testing of that program, and outlines the procedural guide created for developing programs of this sort. Della-Piana's program has 156-frames and includes procedures for generating material, writing haiku and tanka poems, employing different poetic devices and different rhyme, meter, and stanza forms, and revising for greater poetic effect through author and reader analysis. Recommendations for further work in using computer for poetic composition are made. (See Bailey, "Writing Machine," and Marcus for more recent work.)
> [Poetry Writing]

Dembitz, S. (1982). Word generator and its applicability. 1982 International Zurich Seminar on Digital Communications. Man-Machine Interaction, Zurich, Switzerland, 9-11 March 1982. New York: Institute of Electrical and Electronics Engineers, 1982, 159-64.

> The possibility of designing an interactive spelling checker is examined. A word generator which leads to such a checker is based on a statistical model of natural

language. Some experimental results, obtained on samples from Croatian and English, are given.
[Spelling Checkers]

Denee, J. M. (1981). Importance and frequency of entry-level competencies as perceived by word processing supervisors, correspondence and administrative secretaries and word processing educators in Wisconsin. Doctoral dissertation, University of Wisconsin, 1981. Dissertation Abstracts International, 42(4), 1450-A.

A study in which research data were collected on word-processing through surveying word-processing educators, correspondence secretaries, administrative secretaries, and supervisors--so rational decisions on curriculum contents can be made by educators. Dennee uses a revised survey instrument which contains 51 administrative competencies, 51 correspondence competencies, and questions on equipment, history and development of word processing, word-processing instructors, and coming modifications in word-processing offerings. Instructors, correspondence secretaries, supervisors and administrative secretaries (47) differ significantly when rating word processing competencies. Instructors usually consider both correspondence and administrative competencies more important than do the secretaries and supervisors.
[Case Study]

Deutsch, P. L., & Lampson, B. W.(1967) An online editor. Communications of the ACM, 10, 793-803.

Describes QED, an online text editor for timesharing systems. The system was designed to accommodate both novice and expert users. Interesting historically, but few of us would want to go back to this type of editing system which, although far more convenient than its predecessors, would strike the modern word processing writer as incredibly cumbersome.
[Design of Software]

Dickerson, L., & Pritchard, W. H., Jr. (1981) Microcomputers and education: Planning for the coming revolution in the classroom. Educational Technology, 7-12.

Elementary and secondary school focus. Addresses the problem of lack of adequate teacher training in the instructional uses of computers and random "hit and miss" approaches to computer technology in the schools. Public school districts in Florida are surveyed and data are presented to illustrate these problems. No specific mention of writing.

Diem, R. A. (1981). Developing computer education skills: An inservice training program. Educational Technology, 30-2.

Dieterich, D. J. (1972). The magical, mystical, mechanical schoolmaster, or the computer in the classroom. English Journal, 61(9), 1388–95.

> A review of articles and books on uses of computers in education. Nothing specifically on composition instruction, but one monograph on computerized spelling instruction is cited.

Directory of word processing equipment. (1980). Government Data System, 9(5), 26–29.
[Survey of Hardware]

Dollner, I. (1979). Word processing systems: Points to consider. Creative Computing, 5(5), 28–30.

> Pretty fundamental, and brief; might be useful to a novice. The points the author considers relate to data entry, storage and file manipulation, text editing, and formatting considerations (which he calls "reporting"). In the text editing section he discusses line by line editing, global search and replace, automatic reformatting, block movement and hyphenation. Examples are given from IDSWORD, a word processing system developed by Interactive Data Systems, Inc.
> [Survey]

Dukes, T. (1983). How to choose a computer system for your writing center and your home. Unpublished paper presented at the Writing Center Association Fifth Annual Conference, Purdue University.
[Survey]

Dwyer, T. A. (1971). Some principles for the human use of computers in education. International Journal of Man–Machine Studies, 3, 221–222.

Eckols, S. (1980). Report Writer: a COBOL feature that can improve productivity. Fresno, CA: Mike Murach and Associates.

Editors discard red pens for computers. (1982). Communication World, Nov. 1982, 1, 6.

> Mentions WRITER'S WORKBENCH (Bell Labs, Murray Hill, NJ), Writeaids (Westinghouse Electric, Columbia, MD), Computerized Text Editing Processing Program (CACI, Inc., New Orleans, LA), and EPISTLE (IBM, Yorktown Heights, NY), with quotations from the programs' developers.
> [WRITER'S WORKBENCH, EPISTLE]

Elliot, B. (1982). Design of a simple screen editor. Software––Practice and Experience, 12, 375–84.
[Design of Software]

Embley, D., & Nagy, G. (1981). Behavioral aspects of text editors. Computing Surveys, 13, 33–70.

Expert users of text editing systems have been studied extensively by applied psychologists. The article summarizes the "human factors" research on typing, and some studies of pointing devices.
[Design of Software, Human Factors]

Embley, D. & Nagy, G. (1981). Empirical and formal methods for the study of computer editors. In M. J. Coombs, & J. L. Alty, (Eds.). Computing skills and the user interface. London: Academic Press, p. 465–96.

Overview of the basic features of text editors from the point of view of computer science; the formal specification of the "SIMPLE" line editor reveals how such programs are put together. Much of this paper is given to strategies (psychological and computational) which allow editors to be compared, and which evaluate how well and quickly they are learned, e.g., by novice users. An interesting article for people who wish to design text editors or to study how people use an existing editor. See also the review of Anadan.
[Design of Software]

Engel, S. E., & Granda, R. E. (1975). Guidelines for man/display interfaces. (IBM Tech. Report TR00.2720) IBM Poughkeepsie Laboratory.
[Human Factors]

English, W. K., Engelbart, D. C., & Berman, M. L. (1967). Display–selection techniques for text manipulation. IEEE Transactions on Human Factors in Electronics, HFE–B, 5–15.

Dated.
[Human Factors]

Engstrom, J., & Whittaker, J. O. (1963). Improving college students' spelling through automated teaching. Psychological Reports, 12(1), 125–126.

Dated.
[Spelling Checkers]

Epes, M., Kirkpatrick, C., & Southwell, M. G. (1979). The COMP–LAB approach: An experimental basic writing course. Journal of Basic Writing, 2, 19–37.

Description of grammar drill-and-practice that attempts to transfer drill proficiency to actual writing.
[Grammar Drill]

Ettinger, B. (1981). A study of the requirements and business training procedures for word processing personnel with implications for word processing curriculum development in two-year post-secondary institutions. Dissertation Abstracts International, 42(1), 69-A.

Identifies competencies needed by secretaries and supervisors or managers in word processing, investigates company training procedures in word processing, examines word-processing courses of study at various two-year post-secondary schools, and develops guidelines for a word-processing curriculum for such schools. Conclusions: word processing is a growing career field for both sexes in administrative and correspondence roles. Although written primarily with vocational schools in mind, Ettinger does suggest some things college writing instructors need to know: language arts and heuristics will become more important for the average person using word-processing programs.
[Office of Future]

An experiment with casual users. (1981). Which Word Processor or Office of Future System, 2(6), 43-4, 47.

To see if casual use of word processing systems is feasible, the people at WWP borrowed one of the newer, inexpensive microcomputer word processing systems, had a little basic training, kept a copy of the manual, and tried it out on some staff members.
[Case Study]

Fagen, E. R. (1983). Writing/reading: LOGO's systematic learning. The Computing Teacher, 10(8), 43-45.

Reviews Kuchinshas' program which motivates primary school children to write poetry as an example of trying to make the computer as flexible as a pencil, and other, related programs. Claims that the LOGO language will be good for invention, since it easily includes the word and sentence, and might be able to add the paragraph.
[LOGO]

Farrell, E. J. (1967). English, education, and the electronic revolution. Urbana, IL: National Council of Teachers of English. Order No. 18108.

Finn, P. J. (1977). Computer-aided description of mature word choices in writing. In C. Cooper & L. Odell (Eds.), Evaluating Writing. Urbana, IL: National Council of Teachers of English, 69-90.

Discusses a method of determining writing maturity through a combination of the Standard Frequency Index (SFI) and the probability that certain words will appear in a particular writing context. Obsolete technology but suggests possibilities for microcomputer application, particularly for cohesion analysis.

[Semantics]

Fisher, F. (1982). Computer-assisted education: What's not happening? Unpublished manuscript. Reprints are available from the author, Haverford College, Haverford, PA 19041.
[Computer Aided Instruction]

Fluegelman, A., & Hewes, J. J. (1983). Writing in the computer age. Garden City, NJ: Anchor Books.

Foma, E. D. (1981). The effects of massed versus spaced practice on word processing text-editing typing production. Dissertation Abstracts International, 41(9), 4007-A.

Attempts to determine the effects of "massed" and "spaced" practice on word processing with and without a visual screen, in order to make recommendations to community colleges for a curriculum for word-processing courses. Foma finds that word-processing students who meet five periods a week (250 minutes) do not achieve significantly better results than students who meet twice a week (250 minutes also) when their achievement is measured by manipulative exercises and production problems using the IBM Electronic 60 or the Wang System 25. She suggests that either curriculum, massed or spaced practice, for teaching word processing would be effective.
[Case Study]

Fox, M. S., Bebel, D. J., & Parker, A. C. (1980). The automated dictionary. Computer, 13, 35-44.

Preliminary studies conducted for National Institute of Education to discover feasibility of an automated dictionary are outlined, and results given. Discusses future cost of such a system given trends in digital electronics.
[Dictionary]

Frase, L. T. (1967). Learning from prose material: Length of passage, knowledge of results, and position of questions. Journal of Educational Psychology, 58, 266-272.

Frase, L. T. (1969). A structural analysis that results from thinking about text. Journal of Educational Psychology Monograph, 60, 1-16.

Frase, L. T. (1970). Influence of sentence order and amount of higher level text processing upon reproductive and productive memory. American Educational Research Journal, 7, 307-319.

Frase, L. T. (1980). WRITER'S WORKBENCH: Computer supports for components of the writing process. (Bell Labs Technical Report) Murray Hill, NJ: Bell Laboratories.

Describes the development of WRITER'S WORKBENCH. Technical writers were interviewed to discover the components of complex writing activities. Their answers revealed some activities in the stages of writing which could be facilitated by computer, specifically, editing and revising, rather than data collection and planning activities. A broad view of the writing process indicates appropriate use of computer aids in other areas as well, though other papers in the symposium this paper introduces concentrate on editing and revising. Frase's conclusion: "The critical problems that face us are not what computers can and cannot do. They are problems of how well we know and can describe the writing process, editing skills, and the features that characterize good and bad documents."
[Composing Processes, WRITER'S WORKBENCH]

Frase, L. T. (1981). Ethics of imperfect measures. IEEE Transactions on Professional Communications, 24(1), 49-50.

Sound commentary on "readability formulas"--they are reliable, but their validity as a measure of what is hard to read or understand is not known. This note defends the cautious approach which lies behind Bell Lab's WRITER'S WORKBENCH, and points out the limitations.
[Readability, WRITER'S WORKBENCH]

Frase, L. T., Keenan, S. A., & Dever, J. J. (1980). Human performance in computer aided writing and documentation. In P. A. Kolers, M. E. Wrolstad, & H. Bouma (Eds.), Processing of visible language, Vol. 2. NY: Plenum, 405-416.

Although this has a narrow focus on computer documentation, and on the translation thereof, the introductory pages introduce important points about any texts which are drafted and edited on computers. If writers can have access to information (on line) from other sources, they can use parts of early documents readily. In "disciplined writing," such as that which uses a data base, the planning time can increase above the 70% common to "ordinary writing." Writing on an interactive computer will require that "response alternatives" be planned for. Ideally a computer-aided writing system would include a data base of source documents, drafting and editing by the author(s), a way to make drafts available for comment, and ways to tailor parts of comprehensive documents for special users. "Individual methods of producing a draft vary among writers of different experience and ability. Further study of writing processes is necessary to determine optimal conditions for writers at this stage." (p. 408)
[Human Factors]

Frase, L. T., Macdonald, N. H., Gingrich, P. S., Keenan, S. A., & Lollymore, J. L. (1981). Computer aids for text assessment and writing instruction. NSPI Journal, 20, 21-24.

Outlines the WRITER'S WORKBENCH and discusses its general principles. See Macdonald, et al. for the full treatment. WRITER'S WORKBENCH seems relevant for detection (e.g., of spelling errors) and some revision skills, less relevant for production. A final section outlines instructional possibilities--"adjunct," or commentary on texts, "modelling," where students aim for a standard range for the program's features, and "tutorial," where other (unwritten) programs would work on a data base of existing exercises.
[WRITER'S WORKBENCH]

Frase, L. T., & Schwartz, B. (1979). Typographical cues that facilitate comprehension. Journal of Educational Psychology, 71, 197-209.

Fraser, C. W. (1980). A generalized text editor. Communications of the ACM, 23, 154-58.

Editing a text, changing a file directory, and other tasks involve the same functions and commands. However, most systems use different formats and names for the text editor, file maintenance, and program editor. An editor, called s, generalizes the commands for use in all situations. The commands involved are (1) over typing of existing text, (2) + pages, -pages, + lines, and - lines for vertical cursor movement, (3) + search, or - search, (4) delete (the rest of the line, or lines, where the deleted text is remembered), (5) put to put the deleted material at the cursor position, (6) pick to copy deleted material, (7) start for editing a new file and (8) stop to end a session. The number of commands is small enough to be handled easily by most computers' dedicated keys. With such general commands, one relatively small program can be written to serve many functions. Alternatively, the user would need to be alert to the need to figure out editing instructions piece-by-piece, since the convenience of pressing a "delete paragraph" key would be lost.
[Design of Software]

Frenzel, L. (1980). The personal computer--last chance for CAI? BYTE (Computers and Education issue), 5(7), 86-95.

An excellent introduction to what CAI is, for a novice or for humanists who come in through the back door. The author gives a brief history of CAI, sums up pretty fairly the pros and cons, gives background on Control Data's PLATO and on CONDUIT, two popular sources of CAI, and provides a useful glossary.
[PLATO, CONDUIT, Computer Aided Instruction]

Gau, M. J. (1981). Word processing taught at a technical college. The Office, 93(4), 115.

Describes a two-year program in word processing that leads to the degree of associate in applied science at Milwaukee Area Technical College. A one-year

vocational diploma program is also offered. The one-year program trains students for entry-level positions as word-processing operators; the two-year program trains them to operate equipment, make equipment decisions, and perform supervisory and managerial duties. Students receive a minimum of 72 hours of hands-on training with word processors. A rotation plan is used for nine work stations. Students are given a lecture-demonstration once a week with the remaining time spent working with the equipment. A chart to reserve times is used for scheduling by students. The author, an instructor at the school, concludes by offering suggestions to people interested in starting a word-processing training program.
[Office of Future]

Gelsen, D. L. (1981). A CAI "coursewriter" system for the microcomputer. AEDS Journal, 14, 159-68.
[Computer Aided Instruction, Authoring System]

Gerber, A. J. (1980). Modelling the reader's and writer's problem with inhibitor nets. Australian Computer Science Communications, 2(1), 157-172.

Gerhold, G. (1980). Teacher produced CAI. In R. Lewis and E. D. Tagg (Eds.), Computer assisted learning: Scope, progress and limits. Amsterdam: North Holland Publishing Co.

Gerrard, L. (no date) Using a computerized text-editor in freshman composition. Unpublished report, UCLA Writing Programs, Los Angeles, CA 90024.

Preliminary study of two freshman composition classes using Wylbur, an on-line text editing system, for revising essays. Students were selected at random, and did not know they would be working on a computer. Primarily, this is an internal report containing practical information about class and lab management and student responses not just to the machine but to the circumstances surrounding its use. An appended student questionnaire provides some numbers worth looking at as well as comments from students. The report itself is especially useful for those interested in using whatever timesharing systems their school currently has available, as opposed to having microcomputers with word processing software allocated to their use. Gerrard discusses such perennial problems as inadequacy of documentation, need for instruction and warm-up exercises at terminals (as opposed to lectures in class), and the desirability of having tutors or assistants available. The initial results of the study were that students concentrated on using Wylbur to correct mechanical errors and confined themselves to the simpler revising procedures. Composing on-line, because of the inaccessibility of terminals, limited account budgets, and one-hour per session time limits, had to be discouraged. There is some discussion in the conclusion of the report of potential areas of research and classroom use.
[Case Study, Survey]

Gershuny, H. W., & Rosch, D. (1976). Writing as problem-solving in interdisciplinary programs. (ERIC Document Reproduction Service No. ED 126 532)

Outlines a proposed interdisciplinary course linking English and data processing.

Gilb, T., & Weinberg, G. M. (1977). Humanized input. Winthrop, Cambridge, MA.

Gillin, P. (1982) Technical writers get help from editing system. Computerworld, 16(10), 20.

Giovanni, M. E. (1981). Teaching business communications by the traditional writing and the word processing methods--a comparison. Dissertation Abstracts International, 42(2), 514-A.

Designed to see if student attitudes toward a business communication class differ if the traditional or a word-processing method is used. The author studies 70 students enrolled in two sections of Business Communications at Northeast Missouri State University during spring semester, 1980. Conclusions: no statistical differences are apparent on attitude and cognitive achievement as measured by an objective test; the word-processing group does exhibit significantly higher cognitive achievement as measured with the a problem-solving test involving letter writing; no differences exist with student attitudes toward the course. Giovanni recommends, assuming similar results with similar students, that word processing be used to teach writing in business communications.
[Case Study]

Gingrich, P. S. (1980). A measure of text cohesion. Paper presented at the Annual Meeting of the American Educational Research Association, Boston, MA.

Describes computerized evaluation of cohesiveness along the lines of Halliday-Hasan (1976), the assumption being that one should expect more ties within than between paragraphs, through analyzing the closeness of associated words. A method for assessing the cohesiveness of paragraphs is outlined--the program reveals exact repetitions (as morphological variants) of content words--and one small example is given.
[Cohesion]

Gingrich, P. S. (1982). WRITER'S WORKBENCH: studies of users. In The 29th International Technical Communications Conference Proceedings. Boston, MA.
[WRITER'S WORKBENCH]

Glossary of 263 word processing terms. (1980). Datapro Research.
[Glossary]

Glushov, V. (1975). The computer and the arts. Soviet Life, March 1975, 44.

Glynn, L. et al. (1981). Word processing boom. Newsweek, 97, 75.
    [Survey]

Goldberg, M. H. (1972). Cybernation, systems, and the teaching of English: The dilemma of control. Urbana, IL: National Council of Teachers of English.

    Note date, but issues are still relevant.

Goldfarb, C. F. (1981). A generalized approach to document markup. Proceedings of the ACM SIGPLAN, June 1981, 68-73.

    Solely concerned with formatting, but along those lines Goldfarb has a good list of the disadvantages of systematic markups, which (1) do not help to describe the document's content for possible analysis or an information retrieval search; (2) require the author to re-mark the text for each different output device, making cheap draft copies inconvenient if the eventual aim is a high quality, photo-composed text; (3) make it difficult for the author to get the most mileage from competitive typesetting bids, since she's confined to vendors using identical text processing systems; and (4) are complicated to learn, time-consuming, and easy to mess up, especially for complex formatting. The alternative, Goldfarb maintains, is descriptive markup, which identifies textual elements generically, "maps" those elements into position, and processes them. SCRIBE operates along these lines, and requires no procedural markup whatsoever. According to Goldfarb, the Generalized Markup Language (GML) developed by Goldfarb, E. J. Mosher, and R. A. Lorie, is a descriptive markup language with major advantages: it reduces the cost of markup, increases processing options, and saves time in the final production of a book. Additionally, text becomes more amenable to computer analysis.
    [SCRIBE, Typesetting]

Goldstein, I. (1981) Writing with a computer. Proceedings of the 3rd Annual Conference of the Cognitive Science Society, 145-8.

Golub, L. S. (1972). Computer-assisted instruction in English teacher education. In English Education, 1973, 4(2), 92-101.

    Describes the IBM 1500 Coursewriter II designed specifically for instructional purposes by Pennsylvania State University. Article debunks myths about CAI and describes Penn State's program for teacher training, which is mounted in a van and goes from school to school; teachers can learn a unit and then go in and teach it. Two major CAI programs: one for literacy development, which teachers use as preparation for their own classroom activity, and a bilingual program in Spanish and English for elementary and secondary school teachers.

Eventually they intend to provide student modules; the rationale for teacher modules first is that they can be reduced to create student modules, which is easier than the reverse. The article concludes by discussing techniques and strengths of CAI programs, and by making future predictions for CAI use.
[Computer Aided Instruction]

Golub, L. S., & Kidder, C. (1974). Syntactic density and the computer. Elementary English, 51, 1128-1131.

See Kidder and Golub, below.

Good, M. (1981). ETUDE and the folklore of user interface design. Proceedings of ACM SIGPLAN/SIGOA Symposium on Text Manipulation, 34-43.

A good introduction to ergonomics, bringing up problems for users which will be significant to composition theorists, though its user-friendly ideals, as usual, are designed primarily for secretaries, not writers. ETUDE uses a full page, high resolution bit-map display screen with numerous "windows" rather than a conventional CRT (though a conventional CRT screen may be used); it would be interesting, if both types of hardware were available, to compare effects on writers. The designers are working on tailoring an ASCII keyboard for ETUDE; several of their interface improvements rely on specific function keys. Command structure is in simple declarative sentences; Good cites Ledgard, below, on the advantages of natural language command syntax. ETUDE has a special mechanism for abbreviating commands, and several ways to prevent or correct user mistakes: (1) it asks for confirmation, (2) it allows commands to be edited while they're being typed in, as well as to be cancelled after being made or during the operation itself; (3) it allows the user to cancel the results of a command or commands by means of an "undo" key, which prompts a menu list of commands the user has implemented since the beginning of that editing session.

Good addresses the problem of "discretionary users" briefly--middle management personnel using text processors irregularly and needing frequent "on-line assistance" to review; this probably is comparable to the needs of students who only see the word or text processor a week before their papers are due. He discusses the need to provide immediate feedback to the user's commands and clear, well-placed error messages and cites ergonomics experts who stress the importance of responses slow enough to prevent the user from feeling pressured, as well as experts who stress the necessity of speed for interactive, conversational purposes, various hardware considerations, and the need for simplicity--all, of course, in relation to ETUDE. Good's bibliography is a fine resource for anyone interested in designing user-friendly software; we have incorporated all but two or three irrelevant entries here, marked as Good's. The Hammer "ETUDE" article, below, goes into more detail about how ETUDE works, as opposed to its ergonomic justification.
[Bibliography, ETUDE, Human Factors]

Gould, J. D. (1978). An experimental study of writing, dictating, and speaking. In J. Requin (Ed.), Attention and Performance, 7. Hillsdale, NJ: Lawrence Erlbaum Associates, 299–300.

Gould, J. D. (1979). Writing and speaking letters and messages. (IBM Research Report, RC 7528 #32546), available from Thomas J. Watson Research Center, Box 218, Yorktown Heights, NY 10598.

Not directly about word processors. Speaking required 35–75% of the time that writing did, and planning time is two-thirds of total composition time, regardless of output modality, letter complexity, or composition time.
[Case Study]

Gould, J. D. (1980). Experiments on composing letters: Some facts, some myths, and some observations. In Gregg & Steinberg (Eds.), Cognitive Processes in Writing. Hillsdale, NJ: Lawrence Erlbaum Associates, 97–127.

A survey of the connections between cognitive process views of writing generally and the research on letter writing he and others have done. Having discussed the research on such factors as pause times, planning, problem–solving, Gould raises one interesting question about composing and word processors: "... should one risk a 'diversion' while composing, or keep at it, filling in later?" With all the options for revising, we also wonder whether the ease of revision with a text editor might not get in the way of a writer's "forward momentum" in producing written language, particularly for those who go to a "paperless" method of composing. He also briefly mentions the connection between artificial intelligence and text editors, but doubts that this marriage could produce a better letter than a human writer.
[Composing Processes, Case Study]

Gould, J. D. (1981). Composing letters with computer–based text editors. Human Factors, 23(5), 593–606. Also IBM Research Report, RC 8446 (# 36750), 9/2/80, available from IBM Research Center, Box 218, Yorktown Heights, NY 10593.

Letters by research professionals (i.e., quite mature writers), typed (T) on a word-processor were compared with those written (W) in longhand. Gould, in an earlier study, found that these people spend two-thirds of their time "planning" no matter how they get the text down, and no matter how complex the letter is. One third of the time is spent writing or dictating. Variables: planning (reading & pauses), writing/typing, and review of typed text. All T times are longer than W times. The word-processor used requires format commands (e.g., PROSE commands) to be in the text, and fussing with that used up a lot of time. The T letters were modified more often than W letters—that accounts for one fourth of the time difference. If a T letter is more than one screen's worth, it takes more time to skim it than with a W letter.

Comment: It doesn't seem quite fair that the word-processor users got "charged" for letter format, while long hand people didn't (their typists do it for them).

Conclusions--1. This kind of editor may not speed up productivity. 2. Being able to see the whole document may help. 3. Text editors may lead some writers to do a poor job--they will lure them to put things down when they should be planning--folk like gadgets. 4. Think about designing editors which mediate between author and computers better. 5. Electronic message transfer of spoken messages might be better than written transfers. General: this machine is a barrier.

Gould notes that most earlier studies involved a secretary who only followed instructions. This experiment involves the author also doing the typing and editing.
[Case Study, Composing Processes]

Greanias, E. G., & Rosenbaum, W. S. (1978). Automatic spelling verification: Towards a systems solution for the office. IBM Technical Directions, 4(4), 17-23.
[Spelling Checkers]

Grimm, S. J. (1981). EDP user documentation: The missing link. IEEE Transactions on Professional Communication, 24(2), 79.
[Documentation]

Grishman, R., Hirschman, L., & Sager, N. (1975). Computer Science Conference '75. New York: ACM 1975.

Technical. Discusses automatic generation of thesauri; asserts that mechanical syntax analysis, as opposed to statistical analyses of word co-occurrence, can provide information about grammatical relationships and thus improve thesaurus generation. Grishman and Sager's program does just that: it groups nouns according to their co-occurrence, as subject or object, with certain verbs, and verbs according to their co-occurrence with other verbs and nouns. Program was tested on pharmacology texts.
[Syntax]

Halasz, F., & Moran, T. P. (1982). Analogy considered harmful. In Eight short papers in user psychology, T. P. Moran (Ed.), Palo Alto, CA: Xerox PARC, 33-36.

The authors argue that metaphors are not often helpful in explaining how computing systems work. The problem is that extending the parallel, which is often needed to explain all the features of a system, produces an implausible situation with the "ground." Securing a computer file isn't like protecting a folder in a filing cabinet. The "conceptual models" alternative is not worked out very well.

Hallen, R. (1979). Battle of the word processors. Creative Computing. 5(10), 50-52; (11), 48-53.

Differentiates between word processors and text editors, and reviews ED, a line-oriented editor from Digital Research, which you get when you buy CP/M, and EDIT from Technical Systems Consultants. Electric Pencil, designed by Michael Sheayer, is mentioned. TEX and PR, to be used with ED and EDIT respectively, are formatting and printing programs described in Part II.
[Survey]

Halpern, J. W. (1981). Preparing writers to use new communications systems. Simply Stated, 22, 3.

Briefly reviews two projects funded by the Purdue Research Foundation to explore the difficulties of teaching business writers how to dictate more effectively to word processing pools, both under the direction of Professor Halpern. Results of both projects can be found in Proceedings, 1981 National ABCA Conference (Phoenix, 1981), and in the forthcoming dissertation of Sarah Ligget, Purdue University, entitled "Preparing Business Writing Students for Dictation/Word Processing Systems."
[Communication Systems]

Halpern, J. W. (1982). Effects of dictation/word processing systems on teaching writing. In J. Ferrill & S. T. Moshey (Eds.), Business Communication: Academic and Professional Perspectives. Hartford, CT: Aetna Institute, pp. 1-8.

On systems where people dictate (e.g., over the phone) to other people who enter the text on a word processor. Not on the word processor per se.
[Communication Systems]

Halpern, J. W., & Liggett, S. (in press). Computers and composing: How the new technologies are changing writing. Carbondale, IL: Southern Illinois University Press.

The book's research focus is on systems where dictation is channeled to a word-processing (typing) "pool." The research method involves structured interviews coupled with direct observation of the writers' dictation sessions; writers' testimony is judged against current composition theory. One consequence of the research findings is the conclusion that students should learn about new communication systems as part of their writing courses. Among relevant issues are the need to tailor pre-planing to a given system, recognition of their "visual, syntactic, and mechanical conventions," develop cognitive processes to adapt to technological changes. While the monograph does not treat the situation where the writer physically controls the computer, the research design, link between results and theory, and prospects for good research will be important for future studies for

how word processors and their users interact.
[Communication Systems]

Hamilton, D. A., Herzik, A. M., & Nielsen, R. C.   Method for capitalization checking during spelling verification.   IBM Technical Disclosure Bulletin, May 1980, 22(12), 5240.
[Spelling Checkers]

Hammer, M., Ilson, R., Anderson, T., Gilbert, E., Good, M., & Naimir, B. (1981).   The implementation of ETUDE: An integrated and interactive document production system.   Proceedings of the ACM SIGPLAN /SIGOA Symposium on Text Manipulation, 137-145.

A discussion of ETUDE's formatting capabilities in relation to SCRIBE and BRAVO, which it resembles to some degree, notably in the use of tree structure formatting.   See also Ilson entries.
[ETUDE, SCRIBE]

Hammer, J. M., & Rouse, W. B. (1979) Analysis and modelling of freeform text editing behavior.   Proceedings of the International Conference on Cybernetics and Society. New York: Institute of Electrical and Electronics Engineers, 659-64.

Except for a survey of previous research on the human factors invovled in computer text editing, this is not a particularly useful study.   The text editors being studied were TECO and SOS, both of which run on the DEC system-10. Keystrokes of 60 or so "researchers" (a category which is never clearly defined) working on their own programs and "documents" (another amorphous category) were collected without the knowledge or permission of the subjects and a statistical analysis is performed.   The program used to collect keystrokes might be useful to others trying to do the same thing through a mainframe, but the authors do not interpret their results.   The conclusion that "statistically significant differences between editors, between tasks, and among users" exist, but that "differences between editors or tasks were no larger than the differences between users" means little without more information about the operating features of each editor, the types of tasks being performed, and the range of users being studied. An outline of future plans for more specific work is given.
[Human Factors]

Handel, J. (1981).   The new literacy: Programming languages as languages.   BYTE, 6(3), 300-307.
[Computer Literacy]

Handicapped youngsters respond without writing through computer. (1978) Education Update, 12(6).

Hansen, W. J. (no date).   User engineering principles for interactive systems.   AFIPS Conference Proceedings, 39.   AFIPS Press, Montvale, NJ, 523-532.

Hart, G. A. (1981).   Word processor extraordinaire.   Microcomputing, July, 1981, 152-161.

Reviews version 2.26 (now dated) of WORDSTAR, considered one of the best (if one of the most complicated) word processing systems on the market.   Version 2.26 has a file directory which can be displayed either while in a file or while not editing, which previous versions did not have.   WORDSTAR also has cursor movement by "words" as well as by characters.   Automatic formatting and justification as text is typed and help with hyphenation are some other features. Some problems with this—added lengths of files due to special formatting characters, for example—are also discussed.   The reviewer also notes that WORDSTAR is one of the most expensive word processing software packages ($495 at date of publication) available, although ,it eats RAM and disk storage space ravenously, though 8 inch disk drives and/or double density systems accommodate WORDSTAR without much difficulty.   Overall judgment is positive.
[WORDSTAR]

Haselkorn, M. P. (1983).   The computer in the English department.   Paper presented at the Convention on College Composition and Communication, and available from the author, Louisiana State University, Baton Rouge, LA 70803.

Since academia is not a major customer of the computer industry, it's hard to get systems which are tailored to a university environment.   The key is first to understand what computers can do (store and get data, edit, run programs, be interactive, provide type texts, and network), and to link that with what English professors do.   Aside from a brief review of potential applications in the administration of tests and grammar drills, nothing related to writing instruction is presented.
[Grammar Drill]

Haverton, C. (1979).   Text processing versus editing and formatting.   CIPS Review, 3(6), 26-7.

Hawthorne, E. P. (1979).   So, I got a word processor.   Personal Computer World, 2(4), 35-38.
[Testimonial]

Hayes, J. B. (1981).   Word processing: The office of the future is with us today. Creative Computing, 4(4), 119-22.

Introductory article; explains how low-cost microcomputers are increasing the availability of word processing/text editing.   Asserts that a general purpose

microcomputer with word processing software is now a feasible alternative to a dedicated word processor. Then discusses the capabilities of a word processor and lists critical considerations for the user.
[Office of Future]

Hayes, K. C., Jr. (1980). Reading handwritten words using hierarchical relaxation. Computer Graphics and Image Processing, 14(4), 344-364.

Hayes, P., Ball, E., & Reddy, R. (1981). Breaking the man-machine communication barrier. Computer, 14, 19-30.
[Communication Systems]

Hazel, P. (1980). Development of the ZED text editor. Software--Practice and Experience, 10, 57-76.

Discusses an editor developed at the University of Cambridge and reviews its design, features, and implementations. The editor involves a fairly complex command language and is more appropriate for computer specialists than beginners.
[Design of Software]

Hegarty, J. (1980). Text reformatting algorithms. Paper presented at the annual meeting of the American Educational Research Association, Boston, Mass. Technical Report available from Bell Laboratories, Murray Hill, NJ.

Explains how algorithms can help with text format changes (e.g., moving from text to flow-chart or flow-chart to tree diagram) and discusses the effects of such changes. With a drafter document (a set of instructions) and rules for good instructions, three formats were tried--flow chart, numbered list, paragraph. The user starts with one and inserts dot commands to change formats automatically. Going from paragraph to list involves more human decisions and it might help a writer to learn how to do it.
[Typesetting]

Heidorn, G. E. (1975). Augmented phrase structure grammars. In Theoretical Issues in Natural Language Processing, B. L. Nash-Webber and R. C. Schank (Eds.), Association for Computational Linguistics.

Heidorn, G. E., Jensen, K., Miller, L. A., Byrd, R. J. & Chodorow, M. S. (1982). The EPISTLE text-critiquing system. IBM Systems Journal, 21(3), 305-326.

Perhaps the best introduction to EPISTLE, IBM's answer to WRITER'S WORKBENCH, currently available, but some sections are highly technical. It's clearly written, to people who are more interested in its insides, perhaps, than

many composition teachers might be. The article first reviews NLP, the Natural Language Processing system which EPISTLE uses to parse English sentences and which is imbedded within the Yorktown LISP system. NLP works using an augmented phrase structure grammar (APSG) which invokes decoding rules to produce parse trees and diagnose grammar errors, and encoding rules to diagnose style errors. Then user interface is discussed (one of the most useful sections for those not interested in internal affairs), and the color illustrations here are particularly helpful in demonstrating how multiple overlapping windows of different color, size, texture and location work to efficiently provide on-screen help with grammatical and stylistic problems which EPISTLE locates. A substantial section is devoted to EPISTLE's system of dictionary processing, written in EXEC-2 and being improved in PL/I. The possible improvement in spelling checkers which would result as checkers take syntactic information into account, as EPISTLE will eventually do, is briefly discussed, and well as the potential of "fact identification," something which is not sufficiently defined, for indexing, one of the long-range objectives of EPISTLE. A lengthy discussion of grammar parsing follows, which explains exactly what kinds of errors EPISTLE can and cannot diagnose, as well as steps used to detect these errors. How EPISTLE recognizes stylistic errors and what types it recognizes are then discussed, along with the encoding rules NLP uses for style error diagnosis. This is where a detailed comparison to WRITER'S WORKBENCH, once both are more widely available, will be useful. A discussion of long-term plans for EPISTLE follows.
[EPISTLE, WRITER'S WORKBENCH]

Heintz, C. (1982). Two index card programs for the Apple. Interface Age, 7(10), 104-5.

Index card programs allow for multiple and unforeseen access to entries in a data base. "Visi Dex" lets one define a keyword and then search for instances in text which was entered in free form on the screen; it also has aids for building a structured data base. "PFS" is more highly structured, with specified fields, etc.
[Communication Systems]

Henderson, A., & Ward, R. (1982). Customer information about general-purpose computer systems: Unique problems in technical writing. Proceedings of the Conference of the IEEE Professional Communication Society

The problem is the bulk of documentation for computer projects, and the difficulty of getting writers or programmers to do a helpful job. The proposed solution is to have system designers think about users' intended behavior (scenarios) first, so that documentation already matches what users need.
[Documentation]

Hennings, D. G. (1981). Input: Enter the word-processing computer. Language Arts, 63, 18-22.

Hereford, N. (1982). Computers are objects to think with. Instructor, 91, 86–89. (ERIC Document Reproduction Service No. ED EJ 258 782)

Hermann, A. W. (1983). Using the computer as writing teacher: The heart of the great debate. Paper given at the conference entitled The Computer: Extension of the Human Mind, Eugene OR, and available from the author at Teachers College, Columbia University, NY.

> Surveys and approves of composition research that focuses on the process of making the whole text, rather than the "mechanics–usage approach." Notes that little is known about the effects of word processing on writers and writing; frustration in learning how to run the machines, or the location of computers in a noisy "user room" may have harmful effects. Essentially a good "state of the art" review.
> [Survey, Composing Processes]

Hepler, M. L. (Ed.) (1983). CAI in English composition. Pipeline, 8(1).

> A special issue of a publication from CONDUIT, the University of Iowa's nonprofit organization whose purpose is to promote the use of instructional computing at the collegiate level. Contains articles by Shostak, H. Burns, Marcus, Southwell, and Arms. See individual entries. In general, this publication is a useful source of information about a variety of instructional computing, not just writing. CONDUIT also supports faculty across the country who are developing software.
> [Computer Aided Instruction]

Hickey, A. E. (1974). Research guidelines for computer–assisted instruction. Hickey Associates, 42 Pleasant St, Newburyport, MA.

> These guidelines originate from interviews with "14 leading education researchers."
> [Computer Aided Instruction, Survey]

Hiller, J. H., et al. (1969). Opinionation, vagueness and specificity–distinctiveness: Essay traits measured by computer. American Educational Research Journal, 6(2), 271–286.

> A set of 300–word essays on an assigned topic written by 256 students in grades 8–12 were used for the study. The essays were graded by "highly competent" high school English teachers for content, organization, style, mechanics, and creativity. Essays were keypunched and scored by computer. Opinionation and vagueness were found to correlate negatively with the grading criteria, and specificity positively. Hiller cites Page and Paulus, below, and summarizes their work well. He gets his stylistic principles from Strunk and White's Elements of Style.

How this might actually be used to grade essays is not addressed; what is addressed is whether or not computers measuring what Page calls "proxes" (approximate measures) can correlate with human graders responding to the "intrinsic" qualities of the text.
[Evaluation of Writing]

Hillis, P. J., (Ed.) (1980). The future of the printed word: The impact and implications of the new communications technology. Westport, CT: Greenwood Press, Inc.
[Communication Systems]

Hiltz, S. R., & Turoff, M. (1978). The network nation: Human communication via computer. Reading, MA: Addison-Wesley.
[Communication Systems]

Hockey, S. (1978). Text processing in the humanities. IUCC (Inter-University Committee on Computing) Newsletter (Great Britain), 6(3), 8-11.

Hockey, S. (1980). A guide to computer applications in the humanities. Baltimore: Johns Hopkins.

A fine introduction and survey of what is being done in the field. See also Oakman.
[Literary Analysis]

Holder, W. (1982). Software tools for writers. BYTE, 7(7), 138ff.

Description by the developer of THE WORD PLUS, a spelling and stylistic checker. Readers interested in this might also investigate "GRAMMATIK" from Aspen Software. These packages offer scaled-down microcomputer versions of WRITER'S WORKBENCH's STYLE and DICTION programs.
[WORD PLUS, Spelling Checkers, GRAMMATIK, WRITER'S WORKBENCH]

Holdstein, D. H. (no date). Computers and the writing process: Motivation for the technically-oriented student. Proceedings of the American Society for Engineering Education. Available from the author, Computers/Composition Project, Illinois Institute of Technology, Department of Humanities, Chicago, IL 60616.

Holdstein, D. H. (no date). In defense of the practice program: Observations of basic writers. Unpublished manuscript available from the author, Illinois Institute of Technology, Chicago, IL.

Holdstein, D. H. (no date). Motivation and remediation through computerized instruction for writing. Unpublished manuscript available from the author, Illinois Institute of Technology, Chicago, IL.

Holland, M. V. Psycholinguistic alternatives to readability formulas. (Technical Report #12.) Washington, DC: American Institutes for Research, Document Design Project.

A comprehensive review which is bound to affect automatic commentary on written products, aimed specifically at problems involved in extending the application of readability formulas, originally designed for evaluating children's school books, to public documents. The conclusions should be useful for applying readability formulas to help students analyze and revise their own writing.

Holland discusses comprehension problems which do not involve the length and frequency of words and sentences—concrete words, the syntactic content of sentences, and various semantic difficulties, including (a) semantic density (the ratio of content to function words), (b) sentence image concreteness, (c) the semantic integration of word combinations in the sentence, and (d) the semantic distance between two words linked within a sentence. She also spends considerable time on contextual problems in comprehending text, difficulties which transcend mere word or sentence level—how (and how often) sentence relationships are expressed, the text type or genre, what knowledge the reader brings to the text, how clearly the reader understands the purpose of the text, and the text format itself. She recommends the formulas be used as "rough filters" but other more specific and meaningful tests of readability be made for revision purposes, giving examples which are primarily relevant to document designers.
[Readability]

Hollerith, R. (1980). People are different, so why not their work stations? The Office, 92(5), 63–66.

Though written for the general business audience, this article addresses something a composition program using word processing should consider: can we make our students physically comfortable while they write with the machines so they can concentrate on producing text? However, Hollerith's main concern is to improve work station design, and it would be difficult, if not nearly impossible, to implement his suggestions where work stations are shared by all sorts of differently sized and shaped people, even if composition programs had the money needed to invest in the "latest equipment," which they usually don't.
[Human Factors]

Holmes, W. (1982). We saved 191 hours and $2,489.28. Word Processing and Information Systems, April, 1982, 12–14.

Mainly a cost benefit analysis of the "direct entry" method of creating documents (on a Wang System 39 shared logic system) in the Department of Labor, but also

makes some good common sense observations on how the speed of production of a document via word processing allows the writer's ideas to remain fresher as the text is revised and edited.
[Testimonial]

Holznagel, D. (1980). Microsift—a clearinghouse for microcomputers in education. AEDS Monitor, 19(4, 5, 6), 16–7.

Horodowich, P. M. (1981). Developing stylistic awareness on the computer: A tagmemic approach. Paper presented at the annual meeting of the Midwest Modern Language Association, Indianapolis, IN, 1979. (ERIC Document Reproduction Service No. ED 198 530)

Developed to teach stylistic awareness by clause analysis, Horodowich's program uses Hewlett Packard's Instructional Dialogue Author Facility (IDAF) to create what are essentially sentence combining exercises on the computer. Horodowich bases her program in tagmemics; it offers exercises in recognizing types of clauses and practice in subordination of clauses.
[Syntax]

Humes, A. (1979) Post-elementary communication skills architecture: Writing mechanics. Technical Note No. 3-79-13. SWRL Educational Research and Development, Los Alamitos, CA 1979.

Humes, A. (1982). Computer-based instruction on skills for addressing envelopes. Southwest Regional Laboratory Technical Note (2-82/36), available from SWRL, 4665 Lampson Ave., Los Alamitos, CA 90720.

To teach formats to elementary school children, SWRL has developed a program which is operating.
[Elementary Writing]

Humes, A. (1982). Computer instruction on generating ideas for writing description. Southwest Regional Laboratory Working Paper (2-82/03), available from SWRL, 4665 Lampson Ave., Los Alamitos, CA 90720.

Specifications for a program that would lead elementary school children from graphics or pictures on screen (e.g., from videodisc) to description. Some sample screens are illustrated.
[Elementary Writing]

Humes, A. (1982). Computer instruction on sentence combining. Southwest Regional Laboratory Technical Note (2-82/36), available from SWRL, 4665 Lampson Ave., Los Alamitos, CA 90720.

Describes a program which SWRL has developed to teach sentence combining. Eleven lessons have been developed for young children. The lessons are set up so that short kernels are to be combined to give predictable results. Even under those conditions, it is not a trivial task to do the programming. See Lawlor.
[Sentence Combining Exercises]

Humphrey, R. (1982). Two approaches in overcoming the problem of poor writing. The Office, 92(5), 57-58.

Concerned that high-priced word processors do not insure grammatically correct, clear, concise letters and reports, Humphrey documents the efforts of his company--Western-Southern Life--to overcome the problems of poor writing. His goal was more words in less time, but words that indicate an advanced prose style to match the advanced machines.

Hunter, L. (1983). Basic writers and the computer. Focus: Teaching English Language Arts, 9 (3), 22-27.

An anecdotal account of Hunter's experiences with introducing word processing in a college-level remedial writing course. She reports that students had more positive attitudes toward writing and revising and encountered little difficulty accommodating to word processing. Because very little has been done to study the effects of using computers in writing classrooms, Hunter's report and others like it (see Collier above) provide us with starting places for evaluating the successes and failures of computers in writing classrooms.
[Testimonial]

Hylton, C., & Lashbrook, W. B. (1972). Apathetic and neutral audiences: A computer simulation and validation. Speech Monographs, 39, 105-113.

Describes the testing of a program intended to provide a method for audience analysis instruction. The program simulates audiences' responses based on probabilities of audience receptivity toward messages. Lashbrook's unpublished report (1971) describes the program itself.

Illick, P. M., & Taylor, K. B. (1974). Computers & college composition. Journal of Educational Data Processing 11(6), 27-31. (ERIC Document Reproduction Service No. EJ 12 477)

Dated; deals only with recordkeeping.

Ilson, R. (1980) An integrated approach to formatted document production. Unpublished Master's Thesis, Massachusetts Institute of Technology.
[Typesetting]

Ilson, R., & Good, M. (1981). ETUDE: An interactive editor and formatter. (Memo OAM-029) MIT Lab. for Computer Science, Office Automation Group.
   [ETUDE]

Innovative training program introduced for word processors. (1981). The Office, 93(3), 66, 170.

   Kelly Services, Inc. has developed an intensive four-hour course focusing on word-processing concepts (instead of specific systems) to meet the growing demand for word-processing operators. Kelly requires trainees to have typing ability and good language skills. The first part of the course, given in branch offices, familiarizes students with the generic functions of word processing, offering an overview of essential uses. Students use audio and video tapes and workbook exercises. Second, "Guided Discovery Learning" is given at the customer's offices. During a maximum period of four hours, the student becomes familiar with each company's equipment. After the training, Kelly managers regularly communicate with the student's supervisors to gauge the student's progress. Some good information on the current use of word processors in business, and future predictions for the automated office.

Janas, J. M. (1977). Automatic recognition of the part-of-speech for English texts. Information Processing and Management (Great Britain), 13(4), 205-213.

   Describes an algorithm which uses morphological analysis and characteristic word endings as well as syntactic criteria rather than an unwieldy dictionary to assign a word its part-of-speech according to what its surroundings say about it. Has implications for automatic indexing as well as for generation of theseauri. The method is 84% accurate, at least for scientific documents; only 2% were definitely wrong, the rest being defined as "ambiguous" in their classification. Cf. articles by Cherry and Ross.
   [Syntax]

Janello, P. (1983). A study of the computer-related sessions at 1983 CCCC with implications for 1984 CCCC. Report prepared for John Maxwell, Executive Director, National Council of Teachers of English.

   People who led or attended computer-related sessions at the 1983 Conference on College Composition and Communication were questioned about their computer background, perceptions of the conference, and wishes for the future. No demographic trends showed up (i.e., sex, age, professional alliance). About one third of the group were novices; alternatively, about a fourth own a personal computer. The major findings are that 70% would like to see computers being used for "the writing process," and over half hope for "computer-assisted instruction." While the categories are not analyzed further, it seems that the respondents are not especially interested in currently available software. The major recommendation is that future conventions should include hands-on sessions

to evaluate or examine software.
[Computer Aided Instruction]

Jaycox, K. M. (1979). Computer applications in the teaching of English. Illinois Series on Educational Applications of Computers. Urbana: Department of Secondary Education, University of Illinois.

Primarily for high school teachers, but a thoughtful overview with bibliography, references to programs and do-it-yourself exercises. An excellent starting place.
[Secondary Writing]

Jobst, J. (1983). Computers and essay grading. Paper given at 1983 College Composition and Communication Convention, Detroit. Available from the author, English Department, Michigan Technological University, Houghton, MI 49931.

"Grading" in the title includes assessment, supplying explanations about how to remedy errors, and explaining teacher's marks. Jobst reviews automatic assessment strategies by Page and Miller (q.v.). The bulk of the paper describes a program built into the software of the IBM Personal Computer. The dedicated keys are programmed to lead to a teacher-supplied comment, e.g., on comma splices. The teacher prepares a file for the student with a listing of relevant comments. The program also counts error types for the teacher's or student's future reference. Ninety-six students were polled--71% preferred the computer printout to hand written teacher's comments for various reasons, including legibility. This system does not save the teacher any time.
[Evaluation of Writing]

Johnson, D. M. (1980). Skills, knowledge, and attitudes necessary for success in word processing. Dissertation Abstracts International, 40(7), 3717-A.

Attempts to discover what skills, attitudes, and knowledge are necessary for success at various levels of word-processing positions. He interviews supervisors and secretaries to determine further what is needed for success. The approach, described by Glaser and Straus in The Discovery of the Grounded Theory, guides his research and helps develop his theories. Data are coded, analyzed, and categorized using the constant comparative method.

Johnson, P. (1982). Writer's perceptions and what the record shows. Paper presented at the Modern Language Association Annual Meeting, Los Angeles. Available from the Program in Composition and Communication, University of Minnesota, Minneapolis, MN 55455.

Traces how different writers use different composing processes as they switch to word processing. The full report is in Bridwell, Johnson, & Brehe, above.
[Case Study, Composing Processes]

Jones, J. (1980). Primer for R users. <u>MIT Artificial Intelligence Memo #585</u>.

> R is a text formatter.
> [Typesetting]

Jones, P. F. (1978). Four principles of man–computer dialogue. <u>Computer Aided Design</u>, <u>10</u>, 197–202.

Jong, S. (1982). Designing a text editor? The user comes first. <u>BYTE</u>, April 1982, 284–300.

> Jong's main point is not debatable from the writer's standpoint: "software should be designed--and selected--not on the basis of what is most machine-efficient, but on the basis of how well people can use it"; however, some of his recommendations seem biased toward particular systems. Overall, however, a good introduction to the features of text editors.
> [Design of Software]

Jong, S. F. (1983). <u>Word processing for small business</u>. Indianapolis, IN: Howard Sams.

> An interesting book with detailed and comprehensive surveys of hardware, word processing software, and spelling correctors. A nice chapter on "Buzzwords Explained" is also a good general description of how microcomputers work. Probably as good a starting place as any if one is involved with hardware or software purchasing.
> [Survey of Hardware, Survey of Software, Glossary]

Jordan, P., et al. (1976). <u>Community college English lesson index</u>. Plato Publications. Computer-based Education Research Lab (CERL), Univ. of Illinois, Urbana, IL 61801. Order No. US-NSF-C-723. Same title available from National Science Foundation, Washington, D.C. (ERIC Document Reproduction Service No. ED 122 308)

> Brief descriptions of the PLATO lessons available under the Community College English Project, which serve as a teacher's guide for using PLATO courseware in conjunction with other class activities. Each course entry includes a file name (for on-line access), descriptive title, author's name, objective, description, student time, grade level, and subject area, and many include special notes. Courses deal with capitalization, composition, editing, grammar, poetry, punctuation, research, spelling, usage, vocabulary, and miscellaneous. See also Packert-Hall and Burke, below, for a more current description of PLATO.
> [PLATO]

Jostad, K., & Kosel, M. (1981). Search for software. <u>AEDS Month</u>, <u>19</u>, 21–30.

Listing of journals with software reviews and a partial listing of educational software vendors.
[Survey of Software, Bibliography]

Julian, D., Davies, M. (1982). String searching in text editors. Software--Practice & Experience, 12(8), 709-17.

Proposals have been made for fast string-search algorithms that can search for a given pattern without examining every character of the text passed over. These algorithms are effective only if the patterns are long enough, and enough text is traversed to justify the costs of a sophisticated algorithm. Many searches cover substantial amounts of text. However, searches for a single character, moving only a short distance on average are very common. An algorithm must deal with short, single-character searches efficiently.
[Search for Strings]

Kaduda, H. (1982). A double-layered text editor. Journal of Information Processing, 5(1), 1-10.

Describes a text editor called KE (Kernel Editor) which allows a user to define and redefine commands via "microprograms."

Kaplan, S. J. (1982). Natural language in the DP world. Datamation, 28(9), 114-120.

A "natural language system" lets a user interact with the machine in a language such as English or French. The article examines the problems, viability, and desirability of such systems as an alternative to programming languages.
[Design of Software]

Kashyap, R. L., & Oommen, B. J. (1982). Probabalistic correction of strings. Proceedings of PRIP 8. IEEE Computer Society Conference on Pattern Recognition and Image Processing, Las Vegas, NV. New York: IEEE, 28-33.

A probabalistic procedure is suggested for the automatic correction of spelling and typing errors in English texts. The heart of the procedure is a model for the generation of the garbled word from the correct word. The garbler can delete or insert symbols in the word or substitute one or more symbols by other symbols.
[Spelling Checkers]

Kay, M. (1980). The proper place of men and machines in language translation. (CSL 80-11) Xerox Palo Alto Research Center, Palo Alto, CA.

Kearsley, G. P., & Hunka, S. (1979). Documentation in computer-based instruction, SIGUE Bulletin, 13(1), 3-13.

Surveys problems of documenting computer based instruction, considering the need for two levels of documentation: one primarily to catalogue courseware and another for those who will work with the courseware. Discusses manual procedures, self–documenting systems, and post–hoc analysis of programs as means of producing manuals, and the importance of documentation to the development of CAI.
[Computer Aided Instruction]

Keenan, S. A. (no date). Computer projections of the cognitive effects of text changes. Technical Report. Murray Hill, NJ: Bell Laboratories.

Analyzes 60 texts of varying readability for the effects of altering column format on reading behaviors. Alterations in format affect the outcomes of different texts in different ways. Furthermore, changing the computer's model of cognition provides a way of anticipating those differences. Design decisions about typographical format based on "chunks" or meaningful units need a cognitive theory of typography design to do it right. The issue is specifically line length––single vs. double column, etc. Chunks are determined automatically and are smaller for easier texts. Computers are useful to test this sort of theory.
[Readability]

Keller, A. (1980). The design of an adaptive CAI program for the teaching of writing skills. Computer–based instruction: A new decade. 1980 Conference Proceedings. Bellingham, WA: Association for the Development of Computer–Based Instructional Systems, 41–44.

Describes a program which creates and modifies a profile of the student as he or she corrects a set of sentences, and uses this profile to decide what the student needs to learn next. A structural model of a correctly punctuated sentence and a problem–solving model for transforming incorrectly punctuated sentences incorporated into the program make this possible.
[Computer Aided Instruction]

Kenealy, P. (1982). WP software advances rapidly. Mini–Micro Systems. 15(5), 171–80.

A general survey of 75+ word processing packages from over 50 vendors, describing popular features which have become word processing standards; discusses hardware/software "bundles" involving word processing.
[Survey of Software]

Kennedy, T. C. S. The design of interactive procedures for man–machine communication. International Journal of Man–Machine Studies, 1974, 6, 309–334.

Kernighan, B. W., Lesk, M. E., & Ossanna, J. F., Jr. (1978). Document preparation.

Bell Systems Technical Journal (UNIX issue), 57(6), 2115–2135.

Describes programs for document preparation (a term the authors prefer to "text" or "word" processing) within the UNIX operating system: a text editor (ED), programmable text formatters (TROFF and NROFF), macro-definition packages for page layout, special processors for mathematical expressions (EQN) and tabular materials (TBL), and supporting programs including a spelling error detector (SPELL), a voice synthesizer (SPEAK) for proofreading, a program which compares two files and prints differences between them (DIFF), and LEARN, a series of lessons that walk new users through UNIX. ED is line rather than screen oriented, and is meant to be used for programs, data, and documents. TROFF and NROFF are described in some detail. Ease of use and advantages to using a general purpose operating system instead of specialized terminals or dedicated word processors (e.g., a software development facility, the ability to share computing and data resources among a community of users) are briefly discussed.
[Documentation, UNIX]

Kessels, J. L. W. (1980). The reader's and writer's problem avoided. Information Processing Letters, 10(3), 159–162.

Kidder, C. L., & Golub, L. S. (1976). Computer application of a syntactic density measure. Computers and the Humanities, 10, 325–331.

Kiefer, K. E., & Smith, C. R. (in press). Textual analysis with computers: Tests of Bell Laboratories' computer software. Research in the Teaching of English.

Describes how WRITER'S WORKBENCH can be used for stylistic analysis and tutoring with students in freshman composition.
[WRITER'S WORKBENCH]

Kincaid, J. P., Aagard., J. A., O'Hara, J. W., & Cottrell, L. K. (1981). Computer readability editing system. IEEE Transactions on Professional Communications PC-24, 38–41.

Calculates readability scores, flags errant words (probably those not in the dictionary), long sentences, and suggests some replacements.

CRES, Computer Readability Editing System (U. S. Navy's Training Analysis and Evaluation Group--TAEG)--Peter Kincaid, Nora Gregory, Carolyn Trotta, and Charles Guitard and others. Further reports from the group include Kincaid, J. P., Aargard, J. A., & O'Hara, J. W., Development and test of a computer readability editing system (CRES), Orlando, FL: TAEG Report No. 83, March 1980; Cox, R., Computer readability editing system users manual, Orlando, FL: TAEG, June 1982; Kincaid, J. P., Fishburne, R. P., Rogers, R. L., & Chisom,

B. S., Derivation of New Readability formulas (automated readability index, Fog count, and Flesch reading ease formula) for Navy enlisted personnel, Navy Training Command Research Branch Report 8-75, 1975; Smith, E. A., & Kincaid, J. P., Derivation and validation of the automated readability index for use with technical manuals, Human Factors 12(1970), 457-464; Kincaid, J. P., Braby, R., & Wulfeck, W. H., Computer aids for editing test questions, Educational Technology, 1982 (in press).

For a general view and critique of readability formulas, see J. C. Redish, "Readability." Chapter four, in Document design: A review of the relevant research, Felkar, D. B. (Ed.) Washington, DC: American Institute for Research, 1980, pp. 69-94.
[CRES, Readability]

King, G. W. (1982). Style's index compared with readers' scores. Unpublished report prepared by Basic Skills Research Committee and Teaching Resources Center, University of California at Davis.

For the most part, highly technical, and important primarily to those interested in WRITER'S WORKBENCH. The report is intended to discover whether STYLE's indices can predict reader-grader scores on student essays. The study seems carefully designed, and does in fact indicate a high correspondence between STYLE's scores and the evaluations of the two reader-graders whose matched scores for 58 papers were used in the study. But the conclusion that STYLE's indices reveal stylistic variables which influence reader-graders is an unwarranted leap. Reader-graders are looking for qualities of content which STYLE cannot directly measure--a clear thesis, developed ideas, precise, logical thinking. The fact that certain stylistic features are often correlated with these qualities of context does not necessarily indicate that instructors are influenced by these features (though they may well be), only that these features help express sophisticated thought patterns.
[Readability]

Kingman, J. C. (1981). Designing good educational software. Creative Computing, 7(10), 54, 56, 59-60.

Kingman has Developed TRS 80 procedures for designing educational software which can be applied to other computers; suggestions for how to improve courseware quality are made.
[Design of Software]

Kinkead, R. (1975). Typing speed, keying rates, and optimal keyboard layouts. Proceedings of the 19th Annual Meeting of the Human Factors Society, 159-161.
[Human Factors]

Klaver, P. (no date). Computers in writing courses: what can be learned and by whom? Unpublished manuscript, University of Michigan.

Klaver writes for people who have had no exposure to using computers at all, let alone to using them to teach writing. He gives a good analysis of the initial problems that will be encountered by anyone attempting to use a university's large mainframe computer's text editor, but says practically nothing about using "smart" microcomputers not connected to the main system.
[Computer Literacy]

Kleiman, G., & Humphrey, M. (1982). Word processing in the classroom. Compute!, March, 1982.

Kleiman, G., Humphrey, M. M., & Van Buskirk, T. (1981). Evaluating educational software. Creative Computing, 7(10), 84, 86, 88, 90.

Suggests guidelines for evaluation of software, focusing on general principles rather than specific applications.

Kline, D. (1982). Osborne--behind guerrilla lines. Microcomputing, July 1982, 42-50.

A freelance journalist takes an Osborne to Afghanistan and reports on rebels' resistance there by sending his stories through the computer. Probably not useful unless students are involved in a rebel takeover.
[Testimonial]

Kline, E. A. (no date). Computer-aided review lessons in English composition. Paper available from Notre Dame University, Freshman Writing Program, South Bend, IN.

An overview of Notre Dame's programs (traditional CAI) for mastering basic principles about writing--not interactive, not related to text production or editing. Outlines method for designing, accessing, and editing the instructional modules. Examples of modules: discovery procedures, essay coherence, argumentation, description, etc. ". . . unabashedly and unapologetically Aristotelian in bias." See also papers by R. E. Burns, above.
[Computer Aided Instruction, Invention]

Kline, E. A. (no date). Computer-assisted review lessons: English as a second language. Paper available from Notre Dame University, Freshman Writing Program, South Bend, IN.

Particle-to-whole approach for English as a Second Language (ESL) students in traditional CAI format. Categories: phonology, morphology, syntax, punctuation. Reports that the modules were more effective in conjunction with a class, less so as self-instruction modules. Another paper, "Computer-aided Review Lessons in

English Grammar," describes the use of these modules for any students who lack "the rudiments of English grammar."
[Computer Aided Instruction]

Kniffin, J. D. (1982) Computer-aided editing--present and future. Unpublished paper available from Westinghouse Electric Corporation, 10400 Little Pautuxent Parkway, Columbia, MD 21044.

Claims that word processors grew from the increased need for "documentation" in the 1970s. After editing commands were developed, the next programs checked spelling and counted words and syllables for readability measures. The article reviews features of WRITER'S WORKBENCH (Bell Labs), Computer Readability Editing System, or CRES (U. S. Navy) and WriteAids (Westinghouse). Kniffin lists 26 features and it is clear that WRITER'S WORKBENCH is the most comprehensive system of the three. The Navy system can analyze special features in test questions; it can also give simple substitutes for words on a "controlled vocabulary" list. A similar Westinghouse dictionary is longer (1000 words); WriteAids flags all uses of "not" and other negatives. All three programs give statistical data. Writer's Workbench interprets those data against statistical "standards" and it does "objective analysis" of some possible errors. In contrast, CRES and WriteAids do analysis "in context," i.e., between the lines. Users of WRITER'S WORKBENCH and CRES say they improve writing skills and save time. The lists of other features and applications point clearly to the idea that the main point is to improve documentation and technical manuals rather than running English text.
[Readability, WRITER'S WORKBENCH, CRES]

Kolodny, N. H., & Ott, G. T. (1981). Developing computer literacy at a liberal arts college. Proceedings of the 1981 National Education Computing Conference. (NECC) Iowa City, IA: University of Iowa, 59-65.

Describes computer literacy project at Wellesley College.
[Computer Literacy]

Kotler, L. (1982). RSVP (response system with variable prescriptions): Three applications of a computer-based instructional management system for individualizing instruction and advisement in writing and reading. Paper presented at the College Composition and Communication Convention, San Francisco.

Useful paper to examine concrete illustrations of the kinds of feedback RSVP gives to students about their writing problems, strengths. See other reviews (Anandam, RSVP) for elaboration on this system. Exxon supported the development; now widely disseminated.
[RSVP]

Kotler, L. (1982). Some trends in RSVP feedback to English students. TIES (Technological Innovations in Educational Settings), No. 6, 5. (Publication of Miami-Dade Community College.)

> Brief report on RSVP. The publication in which it occurs would probably be useful for anyone interested in an elaborate method of individualized feedback to students. Note that the system is "content and context-free," both a strength and a weakness (from the "interactive" perspective). Feedback about writing is after-the-fact; however, for diagnosis of errors and responses to them, this is definitely the most ambitious project in the country.
> [Evaluation of Writing, RSVP]

Krieter-Kurylo, C. (1983). Computers and composition. The Writing Instructor, 2:4, 174-181.

> Review of computer programs. Covers drill and practice ideas by Wittig and Zoller, Burns' invention program, and aids to the teacher such as RSVP (Anadam, et al.) and Briand. Claims that computers are "no more inhuman than other teaching aids, such as books and records," that they can release teachers from drudgery, individualize instruction.
> [RSVP, INVENT, Invention, Drill and Practice]

Kukich, K. (1983). Design of a knowledge-based report generator. Proceedings of the 21st Annual Meeting of the Association for Computational Linguistics, and available from the author at Carnegie-Mellon University.

> The initial problem is to get a formatted report from a computer data base, such as stock market quotations. The program first infers semantic messages from the data; these messages are turned into phrases (from a set lexicon), which are put together with a clause-combining grammar. Obviously, this is only a pale shadow of what students do when they write, but it does suggest a minimal case.

Kuno, S. (1966). Automatic syntactic analysis. In A. W. Pratt, A. H. Roberts, & K. Lewis (Eds.), Seminar on Computational Linguistics. Washington, DC: U.S. Department of Health, Education and Welfare, 19-41.

> Dated.

Kuno, S. (1970). Computer aids to language instruction. Technical Report, Peace Corps; Language Research Foundation, Cambridge, MA, June 1970.

> Dated; second language learning.

Kwasny, S. C., & Sondheimer, N. K. (1979). Ungrammaticality and extra-grammaticality in natural language understanding systems. Proceedings of the 17th Annual Meeting of the Association for Computational Linguistics, 19–23.

Lampson, B. W. (1979). BRAVO manual. In Altos User's Handbook, Xerox: Palo Alto Research Center.

Lancaster, F. W. (1978). Toward paperless information systems. New York: Academic Press.

Lancaster begins by describing public information–retrieval systems (MEDLARS, etc.), the building of private files (electronic filing cabinet) and electronic mail. The middle chapters explore some of the social and economic issues in technical communication––who reads journals, publication delays, etc. Final chapters explore the feasibility, benefits and problems of paperless systems. An excellent overview and forecast; does not touch directly on what goes into the system(s). [Communication Systems]

Landesman, J. (1983). Writers writing with word processing. Simply Stated, June–July, 37.

Anecdotal accounts, including reflections from the author who is editor of this monthly newsletter from the Document Design Center, American Institutes for Research, Washington, D.C. [Testimonial]

Larson, C. J. (1980). A study of word processing to provide a rationale for educational programs. Dissertation Abstracts International, 41(1), 74–A.

Proposes a rationale for word–processing programs in schools' business courses. Larson interviews 27 word–processing supervisors from the San Francisco area in person and seven by mail using a structured interview guide and concludes: (1) word processing should be offered at the high school level; (2) schools with limited budgets should stress four major areas: word–processing concepts, business English, secretarial skills, human relations; schools with more resources should also stress hardware, data processing, and specialized courses in legal, medical, scientific, and technical typing; (3) all word processing supervisors should expect changes in their systems in the next 3–5 years; (4) these changes include the merger of word processing and data processing, increased use of OCR (optical character recognition) equipment, the establishment of information departments, and greater use of telecommunication equipment. [Case Study]

Lashbrook, V. J., & Lashbrook, W. B. (1974). Applications of computer simulations to interpersonal communication: A selected annotated basic bibliography. New York: ERIC Clearinghouse on Reading and Communication Skills.

Yerkey, below, claims the programs listed deal with "group processes," and are intended to be used as research and instructional tools. Might be worth looking over for audience and conference group heuristics.
[Bibliography]

Lashbrook, W. B. (1971). Program Aristotle: A computerized technique for the simulation and analysis of audiences. Unpublished report, Illinois State University, Speech Communications Research Laboratory.

Lawler, R. W. (1980). One child's learning: Introducing writing with a computer. ACM SIGCUE Bulletin, 14(3), 18-28, Same title in MIT Artificial Intelligence Memo #575, ($1.25).

A very impressionistic study which claims to examine "how one child learned to write in a computer-rich setting" and asserts that "computer access did affect her learning significantly." Lawler gives no evidence that the computer itself was being used in any sense as a unique writing tool.
[Case Study]

Lawlor, J. (1981). Instructional specifications for sentence combining. Southwest Regional Laboratory Technical Note (2-81/08), available from SWRL, 4665 Lampson Ave., Los Alamitos, CA 90720.

Describes a program which sets up sentence-combining lessons and then checks the children's responses. See Humes.
[Sentence Combining Exercises]

Lawlor, J. (Ed.), (1982) Computers in composition instruction. Los Alamitos, CA: SWRL Educational Research and Development.

Publication of the proceedings of a research/practice conference held at SWRL Educational Research and Development, Los Alamitos, April 22-23, 1982. Contains several papers, a reaction to them, and useful appendices. See the individual annotations by author: Shostak, H. Burns, Woodruff, and Southwell.

Ann Lathrop of the SWRL team and the San Mateo County Office of Education gives an introductory overview of elementary school software in "Courseware selection" with useful appendices, one of articles and books evaluating software, another a list of journals, educational and otherwise, which carry software reviews. The article does not refer to word processors.

An anonymous section describes the conferences' courseware demonstrations—of Michael Southwell's CUNY grammar program for developmental writers, and Stephen Marcus's COMPUPOEM (see Marcus, below), both college oriented, and of spelling and sentence combining programs developed by the Minnesota

Educational Computing Consortium and by Irene and Owen Thomas of IOTA, an educational consulting firm, designed primarily for elementary use. The Thomases' work with sentence combining also tries to work around students with few typing skills. Their future plans involve a comprehensive writing program for computers, including prewriting and revising activities and a built-in word processor.

Alfred Bork, University of California at Irvine, is the respondent to these papers; he provides one or two comments on writing but is tangential on the whole and geared primarily to CAI and elementary education.

Joseph Lawlor's "Evaluating textual responses" is provided as an appendix. It describes his sentence combining program which employs a parsing system to distinguish between spelling, capitalization/punctuation, and syntax errors. The success of the program with students and their writing is not evaluated.
[Survey of Software, COMPUPOEM, Sentence Combining Exercises, Spelling Checkers, Computer Aided Instruction]

Ledgard, H., Singer, A., Seymour, W., & Whiteside, J. A. (1980). The natural language of interactive systems. Communications of the ACM, 23(10), 556-563.

Tests an English based text editor against a notational text editor and measures differences in performance on each among inexperienced, familiar, and experienced users. All users performed better on the English based system, and 22 out of 24 preferred the English based system when surveyed and the conclusion of the experiment. All subjects were selected from computer science classes: "inexperienced" had less than 10 hours of computer use behind them; "familiar" users had 11 to 100 hours of experience on computer terminals; "experienced" users could use at least 2 interactive text editors. A sample text was marked with proofreader's marks which were "carefully explained" beforehand. (Students therefore had to master one system of "notation" even before they began with either text editor.)

The authors claim that "a syntax employing familiar, descriptive, everyday words and well-formed English phrases" is better than a mere notational system because "these properties will be easier to learn" (pp. 556-7), but almost no time is spent explaining what is meant by such attributes. The English-based system's chief advantage is that it employs adjectives and prepositions to elaborate on basic commands instead of arbitrary symbols for what have previously been considered lightweight words; the English-based system does not employ technical jargon such as "buffer" either, but uses a more descriptive term like "holder." Arbitrary symbols for some nouns (usually jargon) are occasionally used in the notational system; e.g., "*" for current line and "$" for buffer. Users could abbreviate editing commands on both systems using the first letter of each command, thus removing any advantage of speed the notational system might have had. The experiment does not attempt to discover how many subjects chose to use abbreviated commands on either system.

A good study, on the whole, though only someone used to the complicated notational systems for editing which universities have inherited from their computer science departments would consider these conclusions revolutionary. [Design of Software]

Ledgard, H. F., Whiteside, J. A., Seymour, W., & Singer, A. (1980). An experiment on human engineering of interactive software, IEEE Transactions on Software Engineering, SE-6(6), 602-604.

See Ledgard et al., above.
[Human Factors]

Lee, L. S. (1981). Converting paper records to micromedia--Part 3. Journal of Systems Management, 32(10), 39-42.

Summarizes how to implement a system for retaining records and how to maintain equipment. This could be applied to a writing program to store student writing, effective handouts, and other class materials on disks for later use by others.
[Communication Systems]

Leibowicz, J. (1982). CAI in English. (ERIC/RCS Report No. 429); English Education, 14, 241-47.

Survey of developments between 1978 and 1982. Points to the expanded role of interactive over batch computers, but notices that most programs are "drill and practice" (or, more elegantly, "tutorial") which are obviously mechanical. Favorable comments are given to the work by Burns, Wresch, and Schwartz. One problem is that even the best of the lot has no consistent record of improving writing quality.
[Computer Aided Instruction, Drill and Practice]

Leikam, G. E., & Wierwille, R. L. (1982). Conditional means for word processing display terminals. IBM Technical Disclosure Bulletin, 24(8), 4110-12.
[Design of Hardware]

Lemmons, P. (1981). Five spelling-correction programs for CP/M based systems. BYTE, 6(11), 434-48.

Discusses MICROPROOF, THE WORD, SPELLGUARD, MICROSPELL, and WORDSEARCH.
[Spelling Checkers]

Levin, J., & Borula, M. (1981). Microcomputer-based environments for writing: A writer's assistant. Unpublished manuscript. San Diego: University of California.

Levin, R., & Doyle, C. (1983). The microcomputer in the writing/reading/study lab. T. H. E. Journal, 10(4), pp. 77–100.

> Introductory. One community college's experience of the potential of microcomputers (especially of the word processor's capabilities) for writing, reading and research. They don't say what equipment they're using, and base their comments on student improvement largely on impressions. Has some anecdotal value as an eye-opener, but otherwise a little naive.
> [Testimonial]

Levison, M. (1982). A programmable text-editing system. Software--Practice and Experience, 12, 611–21.

> Describes the "IVI" editor developed at Queen's University (Kingston, Ontario), which can be programmed to do various editing routines. "Macros," i.e., series of commands that are to be revised, can also be built and stored. An example is a macro to define the format of a business letter. The editor can also cue the computer programmer to fill in syntactically accurate code, and it can be used for a (small) structured data base.
> [Design of Software]

Levison, M. (1983). Editing mathematical formulae. Software--Practice and Experience, 13, 189–95.

> Most systems that edit formulas ask the user to type in a line of characters (including special formatting symbols); a program sets up the printer layout. This approach has the writer build the formulas on the screen, with help of a few subroutines such as "integrate," and "superscript." It is thus analogous to a text editor.
> [Typesetting]

Lewenstein, M. (no date). Re-designing the wheel: Using computer-aided instruction in journalism teaching. Unpublished paper, available from the author. Department of Communication, Stanford University, Stanford, CA 94305.

> Informal working paper describing what's available for writing instruction in journalism. Reviews some familiar ground (WRITER'S WORKBENCH, PLATO, WANDAH from UCLA) and systems developed in several journalism schools around the country.
> [Journalism. PLATO, WANDAH, WRITER'S WORKBENCH]

Lewis, J. W. (1975). TREE: An interactive system for editing tree structures. Computers & Graphics (Great Britain), 1(1), 65–68.

> Describes a system for editing data trees using principles drawn from text processing. Syntax trees and decision trees for LISP programs can be entered and

changed quickly using TREE; the program is coded in PDP 10 FORTRAN IV and runs on many cheap graphics terminals.

[Programming]

Lewis, R., & Tagg, E. D. (Eds.). Computers in education. AFIPS Press.

Lippold, W. A. (1978). Whys and hows of WP system flexibility. Datamation, 24(9), 165-6.

Long, J. (1976). Visual feedback and skilled keying: Differential effects of masking the printed copy and the key board. Ergonomics, 19, 93-110.

[Human Factors]

Luehrmann, A. (1980). Computer literacy--a national crisis and a solution for it. BYTE, 98-102.

[Computer Literacy]

Luehrmann, A. (1981). Computer literacy. EDUCOM Bulletin, 16(4), 14-15, 24.

In surveying adjustments colleges and universities will have to make because of the increase in computer literacy among high school students, Luehrmann comments that "the majority of college entrants will be experienced in the uses of word processing software as a routine aid to writing. Word processing software might be resident on a micro, mini or mainframe, and might be available to them personally or through their high schools. They will expect similar tools to be available in the colleges of their choice." Luehrmann goes on to discuss the desirability of the microcomputer laboratory, and the need for liberal arts faculty to apply and teach computing concepts. He suggests "in service training" for these faculty as "the best source of professional development in computing within a university."

[Computer Literacy]

Lukas, T. (1981). How to set up an electronic bulletin board. T. H. E. Journal, 8, 50-3.

[Communication Systems]

Lycklama, H. (1978). UNIX on a microprocessor. Bell Systems Technical Journal (UNIX issue), 57(6), 2087-2101.

Describes the implementation of UNIX on a personal computer, the DEC LSI-77. Text processing using ED (the editor), ROFF and NROFF (formatters) is briefly discussed. A fairly technical article.

[UNIX]

Macdonald, N. H. (1979). Pattern matching and language analyses as editing supports. Paper presented at the American Educational Research Association Meeting. Technical Report available from Bell Laboratories, Murray Hill, NJ.

Overview of WRITER'S WORKBENCH, with more examples than Macdonald, et al. (1982), below.
[WRITER'S WORKBENCH]

Macdonald, N. H. (1982). The WRITER'S WORKBENCH programs and their use in technical writing. The 29th International Technical Communications Conference Proceedings. Boston, MA.
[WRITER'S WORKBENCH]

Macdonald, N. H., Frase, L. T., Gingrich, P. & Keenan, S. A. (1982). The WRITER'S WORKBENCH: Computer aids for text analysis. IEEE Transactions on Communication (Special Issue on Communication in the Automated Office), 30, 105–110.

WRITER'S WORKBENCH does proofreading, stylistic analysis, and gives reference information. Proofreading includes: spelling (30000 word dictionary, no updating), punctuation (periods, quotation marks, and semicolons) capitalization after periods, unbalanced parentheses and quotation marks, same word twice in a row, undesirable phrases ("bring to a conclusion" for "conclude"), split infinitives (using –ly adverbs). STYLE includes: readability formulas, word and sentence lengths, simple vs. complex sentences, percentage of passive verbs, nominalizations, and sentences which start with expletives. The output is a table, but text values can be compared to user-set norms. (The authors note that this may not affect the writer's style.) It can find instances of the verb be.

An organization program will isolate the first and last sentences of paragraphs to see if they make sense. A sexist-language program picks up "man," etc. Abstract words (from a list of 314 based on psychological research) are flagged. See Macdonald, "Pattern matching and language analysis as editing supports" (above), for a companion piece with more illustrations.
[WRITER'S WORKBENCH, Spelling Checkers]

Macrorie, K. (1970). Percival: The limits of behaviorism. Media Method Explorations in Education, 6(7), 45–6. (ERIC Document Reproduction Service No. EJ O17 252)

Historically interesting. Discusses the "dehydrated manner of producing writing which is fostered by English teachers" evaluation standards; prompted by an examination of Page and Paulus's "The Analysis of Essays by Computer," below.
[Evaluation of Writing]

Mandell, M. (1981). Word-processing packages for mainframes, minis, and micros. Computing Decisions, 13(1), 76–7, 79–80, 82, 86, 88–90.

A way to ease into word processing is to buy one, but one may ultimately need more computing power or space.
[Survey of Software]

Maner, W. (1978). Generative CAI in Aristotelian logic. In R. Prather (Ed.), Proceedings of the 1978 Conference on Computers in the Undergraduate Curricula. Denver, CO: University of Denver.
[Computer Aided Instruction]

Mann, W. C. (1975). Why things are so bad for the computer-naive user. (Technical Report ISI/RR-75-32) University of Southern California Information Sciences Institute.

[Human Factors]

Mann, W. C. (1977). Man-machine communication research: Final report. Marina del Rey, CA: Information Sciences Institute of the University of Southern California.
[Communication Systems]

Marcus, S. (1981). COMPUPOEM: A computer writing activity. South Coast Writing Project Newsletter, 1(3), 3.

This gives the most complete treatment of COMPUPOEM, including a listing and several student examples. The program gives cues--"Type in a noun," "Now an adjective," "A prepositional phrase." These are mapped onto a phrase-structure map of the short poem. A second round asks for phrases as substitutes for the individual words.
[COMPUPOEM]

Marcus, S. (1981). Teaching writing skills using microcomputers. In Proceedings, Conferences on Computer-Using Educators.

A simple overview of COMPUPOEM.
[COMPUPOEM]

Marcus, S. (1982). COMPUPOEM: CAI for writing and studying poetry. The Computing Teacher, March 1982, 28-31.

An informative blurb about COMPUPOEM. Marcus spends a lot of this short article outlining the composing process for a general audience; it's not really clear that his "computer assisted writing activity" is intrinsically more process-oriented, although he makes a case here for its being different from "poetry" programs of the past, and notices some interesting things about the writing processes of students using COMPUPOEM to produce first drafts of poems. Whether the parts-of-speech prompts which COMPUPOEM provides can genuinely be

considered a poetry writing heuristic as Marcus claims is perhaps debatable. His
students seem to do impressive amounts of prewriting and revising of their poems,
but how much the CAI fosters this, and how much is dependent on the
philosophy of the instructor, remains unclear.
[COMPUPOEM]

Marcus, S. (1982). COMPUPOEM: A computer-assisted writing activity. The English
Journal, 71(2), 96-99.

  See Marcus, passim.
  [COMPUPOEM]

Marcus, S. (1983). The muse and the machine: A computers and poetry project.
Pipeline, 8(1), 10-12.

  An illustration of a student's work Marcus's COMPUPOEM program.
  [Poetry Writing, COMPUPOEM]

Marcus, S. (1983). Real-time gadgets with feedback: Special effects in computer-
assisted writing. The Writing Instructor.4(2), 13-21.

  Using computers in prewriting, group feedback, writing and revision; classroom
  techniques and effects.

Marcus, S., & Blau, S. (1982). Not seeing is relieving: Invisible writing with
computers. Educational Technology, manuscript submitted for publication.

  Briefly reviews results of a study to determine the effects of "blind writing," a
  technique for early invention drafting which records what students type in, but
  prevents them from seeing (and thus rereading or editing) what they have
  produced. Authors claim this approach helps students see how premature editing
  interfered with their composing processes.
  [Case Study, Composing Processes]

Margulies, F. (1979). Technological change: Its impact on man and society. In
Man/Computer Communication, 2, Infotech State of the Art Report, Maidenhead,
England, 251-261. (From Good's bibliography; see his ETUDE article, above.)

Marling, W. (1983). What do you do with your computer when you get it? Focus:
Teaching English Language Arts, 9(3), 48-53.

  A brief report on Marling's programs, WRITER, GRADER, and READER, which
  allow a teacher to respond to student writing done on a microcomputer (now the
  IBM-PC). The programs are mainly useful for "boilerplate" commentary and

explanations, the kinds of things teachers find themselves writing repeatedly on student papers. The programs also assist in record-keeping by recording frequencies of errors in a student's essays and by providing students with summaries of all the commentary they have received. but Marling is careful to point out that they don't save any time, in fact they take more time. He also shares news of other programs under development and helpful suggestions for writing teachers based on his experiences with writing software.
[Evaluation of Writing]

Martin, T. H. (1973). The user interface in interactive systems. In C. A. Cuadra (Ed.), Annual Review of Information Science and Technology, 8. Washington, DC: American Society of Information Science, 203-219.

Defines an interface as a physical/conceptual structure that both channels and facilitates communication. Dated.
[Human Factors]

McCormick, E. J. (1976). Human factors in engineering and design. New York: McGraw-Hill.
[Human Factors]

McIlroy, M. D. (1982). Development of a spelling list. IEEE Transactions on Communications, 30, 91-99.

Describes how the UNIX spelling checker (SPELL) works, how the words were selected, refinement of the spelling checker, and how the 30,000 English words which made up the list, reduced by stripping prefixes and suffixes, hashing, and data compression, were squeezed into 26,000 16 bit machine words. The checker may be used on minicomputers.
[Spelling Checkers]

McKenzie, A. T., et al. (in press) A grin on the interface: Word processing for the academic humanist. New York: Modern Language Association. Preprint available from Department of English, Purdue University, West Lafayette, IN 47907.

Enthusiastic and non-technical introduction which is supposed to provide the literary scholar with inspiration to buy or use a word processor, and with a rationale for trying to get one in the department's offices. Includes chapters on cost saving from having a departmental computer, comparisons of systems, and examples of scholarly applications. One appendix gives an introduction to some special features of WORD 77, WORDSTAR, and SUPERSCRIPT. Nothing directly on composition instruction.
[WORDSTAR, SUPERSCRIPT, WORD 77]

McLean, R. S. (1980). School microcomputers: Literacy in an information age.

Microcomputers in Secondary Education: Proceedings of the IFIP (International Federation for Information Processing) TC 3 Working Conference.   Paris, France, 83-88.

McMahon, L. E., Cherry, L., & Morris, R. (1978).   Statistical text processing.   Bell Systems Technical Journal (Unix issue), 57(6), 2137-2154.

    A technical article on UNIX facilities for statistical studies of English text. Summarizes some studies made at the level of characters, character-strings, and English words, and provides a case study of how to use the UNIX tools for examining the statistics of English.   Claims that the basic concepts of UNIX programming are especially useful for collecting statistics, that the C language, due to its good character manipulation facilities, is convenient to use, and that the frequency of UNIX use for document preparation ensures that a large body of text for practicing and sharpening these tools will always be available. [UNIX]

McWilliams, P. A. (1982).   The word processing book: A short course in computer literacy.   Los Angeles: Prelude Press.

    Pleasant, enthusiastic book.   Includes a long brand-name buying guide to software, printers and computers.   In addition to word processors, the software reviewed includes "THE WORD" and "GRAMMATIK".   Interesting warnings about the difficulties or impossibilities of using 1982 model Ataris, Apples, Radio Shack TRS-80s for word processing.   You can get an updated guide by writing to McWilliams, Box 69773, Los Angeles.
[GRAMMATIK, THE WORD, Survey of Hardware, Survey of Software]

McWilliams, P. (1982).   Writing poetry on a word processor.   Popular Computing, 1(4), 38-40.

    Anecdotal; despite the apparent incongruity, poets are now using word processors to compose their poems.
[Poetry Writing, Testimonial]

Menkus, B. (1981).   Why hasn't word processing worked better?   Journals of Systems Management, 32:11, 38-39.

    Word processing only produces documents; it does not distinguish whether the document is valuable or not, so it only affects secretarial or clerical activities. The problem is to rethink the value of the documents themselves.

Merrit, F. (1974).   Audience analysis: A computer assisted instrument for speech education.   Unpublished paper presented at the Convention of the Southern Speech Communication Association.

Merrit, F. Wheately, B. & Cash, W. (1972). Audience analysis: A computer-aided instrument for speech education. Today's Speech, 20, 49-50.

Michael, G., & Sliger, M. (Eds.) (1976). Language arts routing system (LARS) instructor's manual. Community College English Project. PLATO Publications, University of Illinois, Urbana, IL.

    See Jordan, above, and Packert-Hall and Burke, below.
    [PLATO]

Miller, G. (1979). Automated dictionaries, reading and writing. Chairman's report of a Conference on Educational Uses of Word Processors with Dictionaries, June 14-15, 1979. Washington: National Institute of Education, U. S. Department of Health, Education and Welfare.

Miller, L. A. (1980). Project EPISTLE: A system for the automatic analysis of business correspondence. Proceedings of the First Annual National Conference on Artificial Intelligence, Stanford, CA, 280-282.

    The EPISTLE system is intended to provide the business executive with computer processing of correspondence in the office. Applications will include the abstraction of incoming mail and a variety of critiques of newly-generated letters, all based on the capability of understanding the natural language text at least customary business communication. Sections of the paper describe the background, the planned output, and the implementation. (See Heidorn, above, for additional discussion.)
    [EPISTLE]

Miller, L. A. (1982). Natural language text [sic] are not necessarily grammatical and unambiguous. Or even complete. In Proceedings of the Association for Computational Linguistics.

    A brief report based on Miller's work with the EPISTLE system which outlines how that system treats unrecognized words, lapses in its own grammar (as opposed to ungrammatical input or fragments), and multiple parses.
    [Syntax]

Miller, L. A., Heidorn, G. E., & Jensen, K. (1981). Text-critiquing with the EPISTLE system: An author's aid to better syntax. AFIPS Conference Proceedings, May 1981, 50, 649-655. Paper originally presented at the National Computer Conference.

    EPISTLE is an experimental system designed at the IBM Thomas J. Watson Research Center in New York for critiquing business correspondence. Primarily it makes grammatical judgments ("Type I" errors), although attempts are in progress to make it produce text feedback ("Type II" acceptability critiques) similar to that

of WRITER'S WORKBENCH. Unlike WRITER'S WORKBENCH, however, which relies on morphological and word-pattern analyses, EPISTLE is parser-based. (Miller does not, at least in this paper, present any comparison.) EPISTLE is built upon NLP, a general purpose Natural Language Processor embedded in LISP, a computer language often used for linguistic research. The parser works syntactically, based on the parts of speech and inflectional characteristics of words, and not on any semantic considerations. It focuses on the actual surface structure of a sentence as the key syntactic element, not on a hidden deep structure. The system's grammar is a collection of decoding rules known as an Augmented Phrase Structure Grammar. Details of the system's operations and future critiquing objectives are discussed.
[EPISTLE, WRITER'S WORKBENCH, Syntax]

Miller, L. A., & Thomas, J. R. (1977). Behavioral issues in the use of interactive systems. International Journal of Man-Machine Studies, 9, 509-536.

A theoretical-review article that seeks to identify behavioral issues related to various uses (including text editing) of interactive systems by non-specialists. In the section on text-editing, the authors try to define the characteristics of a "well-designed" text editor in terms of its editing and searching capabilities. The authors conclude that a well-designed text editing program provides efficient searching, block-moving, and string-replacing capabilities. Somewhat dated, since most text editors in 1982 have such capabilities.
[Human Factors]

Miller, L. H. (1977). A study in man-machine interaction. AFIPS Conference Proceedings, 46, 409-421.
[Human Factors]

Miller, R. B. (1971). Human ease of use criteria and their tradeoffs. (Technical Report TR00.2185) IBM Poughkeepsie Laboratory.
[Human Factors]

Misek-Falkoff, L. D. (no date). Computing and composition: Structured programs Are outlines, outlines Are programmed structures. Yorktown Heights, NY: IBM, T.J. Watson Research Center.

The author discusses the similarities between structured computer programs and familiar principles of organization in natural language discourse. Newer breeds of "writing" may not vary greatly from other forms of composition; both programming and prose composition may be addressed in a general curriculum firmly grounded in rhetoric.
[Design of Software]

Misek-Falkoff, L. (1981). Data-base and query systems: New and simple ways to gain multiple views of the patterns in text. (IBM Research Report RC 8769 (#38450), 3/30/81.) Available from the author.

>While not directly related to writing with computers, the examples of computer-assisted literary analysis suggest possibilities for studying textual features in student writing using on-line, interactive approaches, especially since compositions produced via word-processing are already "machine-readable." [Literary Analysis]

Misek-Falkoff. L. (1982). Computing and composition: The new field of software linguistics. (IBM Research Report RC 9421 (#41156), 4/19/82.) Available from the author.

>Misek-Falkoff uses analogies from natural language to describe and analyze software programs as "texts" in the field of "software linguistics." Her stimulus was a statement by Maurice Halstead suggesting that software science could shed some light on natural language and linguistics in ways that might reveal some basic canons of the writing arts. While her paper goes the other way, she concludes that the transfer will probably be bi-directional.
>[Design of Software]

Moe, A. J. (1980). Analyzing texts with computers. Educational Technology, 20(7), 29–31.

>A very good introduction to the various methods of computerized text analysis, including those which examine vocabulary, word strings, sentence and syntactic complexity, and readability. A concise review of the literature and a lengthy bibliography is provided. Material is applicable to analyses of student texts as well as to those of literary texts, but specific classroom applications are not treated.
>[Bibliography, Evaluation of Writing]

Moran, C. (1983). Word processing and the teaching of writing. English Journal, 72(3), 113–115.

>A high school English teacher's testimonial for other teachers on the benefits of word processing for the future. Anecdotal account of how his family—including a professional writer-mother, an English-teacher father, a tenth grader and an eighth grader—uses their word processor. Admittedly not a random sample, but typical of converts' accounts.
>[Testimonial]

Moran, T. P. (1981). An applied psychology of the user. Computing Surveys, 13, 1–11.

>Introduces a special issue of Computing Surveys with five papers that explore user behavior with the hope of improving the hardware or programs on one hand, or

optimizing what the user does, or both. If the user's psychology is studied carefully, the tendency of some system designers to work egocentrically may be overcome. We need to know the user's goal (presumed to be rational), the system's task structure (what's possible), what the user knows, and her or his "processing limits" (e.g., on memory). The novice is contrasted with the expert, for whom interacting with the computer is a routine cognitive skill. A key element is the user's conceptual model of the machine, which needs to be directly addressed by system designers.
[Human Factors]

Morgan, C. (1980). Nestar lets personal computers talk to each other. OnComputing, 2(1), 28-31.
[Communication Systems]

Morris, R. & Cherry, L. L. (1975). Computer detection of typographical errors. IEEE Transactions on Professional Communications, PC-18(1), 54-64.
[Spelling Checkers]

Motto, J. W. (1981). The next step: The use of the microsynergistic (microcomputer cluster) in education. Proceedings of the NECC 1981. National Educational Computing Conference. Iowa City, IA: University of Iowa, 24-33.

Describes design and implementation of a six unit network of personal computers interfaced to the main academic computer in a small undergraduate college. Commercially available hardware is used.

Mudur, S. P., & Narwekar, A. W. (1979). Design of software for text composition, Software--Practice & Experience (Great Britain), 9(4), 313-23.

Text composition here means setting type.
[Typesetting]

Myers, W. (1980). Computer graphics: The human interface. Computer, 13(6), 45-54.

Computer graphics and word processing are everyday tools now, and their design is being influenced by this.
[Design of Software]

Nahin, P. J. (1979). A computer that writes science fiction (using RUNOFF, the information processing system). Analog Science Fiction/Science Fact, 99, 93ff.

Naiman, A. (1982) Introduction to WORDSTAR. Berkeley: Sybex.

A clear discussion of all the features of WORDSTAR, although not a "teaching" introduction. Aside from a very short first lesson, the beginner is not given anything to try (that lesson, incidentally, is error-free, so the beginner doesn't get a feel for corrections.) Excellent summary of commands in Appendix D, with charts, etc., again keyed to the menus.
[WORDSTAR]

Nancarrow, P. R. (1982). Integrating word processors into a freshman composition curriculum. Paper presented at the Modern Language Association Annual Meeting, Los Angeles. Available from Program in Composition and Communication, University of Minnesota, Minneapolis, MN 55455.

Attempts to provide a working model for a freshman writing course using word processors, based on the author's experience teaching Freshman English using microcomputers running WORDSTAR. Issues considered include the word processing/writing lab itself, time requirements for students using the machines, methods of incorporating word processing instruction into a writing context, student reactions, and the particular needs of freshmen. The author asserts that "since freshman writers are generally less experienced problem solvers than upperclassmen, have not had as much exposure to computers, and rarely have developed efficient writing habits, they usually need greater initial supervision in using the machines, a more controlled exposure to the various word processing options available to them, and clearer connections made between the word processor's capabilities for changing text and the demands of the writing process itself." Several sample exercises supplementing the text being used in the course, Jeff Rackham's From Sight to Insight, are provided; they focus on prewriting, "voice" flexibility, tightening prose, searching and replacing passive constructions, and global revision.
[WORDSTAR, Computer Aided Instruction]

Nancarrow, P. R., Ross, D., & Bridwell, L. S. (1982). Word processors and the writing process: An annotated bibliography. Unpublished manuscript, available from the English Department, University of Minnesota, Minneapolis, MN 55455.

Preliminary version of this bibliography.

Nelson, H. (1981). Another industry giant takes a micro step. Microcomputing, 94-98.

Describes the Xerox 820 Information Processor. Though the Xerox 820 "is not designed to be a home or hobbyist's computer," Nelson claims it is "a good choice for anyone who has to do a good deal of writing" (p. 98). A fairly informative review, though the Xerox 820 has since been upgraded and the IBM-PC has captured much of its market.
[Survey of Hardware]

Nelson, T. H. (1980). Replacing the printed word: A complete literary system. Information Processing 80. Proceedings of the IFIP Congress 80. Amsterdam, Netherlands: North-Holland, 1013-23.

> Discusses the replacement of paper as a medium for distributing written material, and describes a system for storage and retrieval of text; links and windows provide "access pathways" to older material. The system necessarily involves a great deal of "data fragmentation," which the author claims can be made tolerable by quick proprietary algorithms. Technical.
> [Design of Software]

New directions for word processing. (1980). San Jose, CA: Creative Strategies International.
> [Survey]

Newell, S. B. (1982). Introduction to microcomputing. New York: Harper & Row.

> Not exactly the rank beginner's handbook, but a thorough introduction to the way a microcomputer works, beginning with a discussion of basic definitions (e.g., I/O, RAM, microprocessor) and proceeding to increasingly more technical discussions of algorithms and flowcharts in programming, loops, subroutines, system configurations, etc. Very useful for the hardcore addict; not necessary for those just interested in how to put word processing software into a disk drive so they can write.
> [Design of Software]

Newkirk, R. L., & Suttie, I. P. (1972). Computer-assisted instruction (CAI) sequence writing: A valuable learning experience for students. Saskatchewan Journal of Educational Research and Development, 2(2), 41-5. (ERIC Document Reproduction Service No. EJ 058 193)

> Note the date.
> [Computer Aided Instruction]

Nichols, P. (1982). Word processing program prepares students for the automated office. Information and Records Management, 16(2), 38, 39, 43.

> Outlines the word-processing program at Murray State University. Admittedly, most of this applies to technical or vocational schools; however, as college composition programs offer more and more technical writing courses, this article could be useful.
> [Office of Future]

Nickerson, R. S.,& Pew, R. W. (1971). Oblique steps toward the human-factors engineering of interactive computer systems. Appendix to Mario C. Grignett, et al.,

BBN Report No. 2190, Information Processing Models and Computer Aids for Human Performance. (NTIS No. AD 732 913)
[Human Factors]

Nievergelt, J. (1980). A pragmatic introduction to courseware design. Computer, 13(9), 7-14, 16-21.
[Design of Software]

Nivat, M. (1979). Infinite words, infinite trees, infinite computations. In J. W. De Bakker, & J. Van Leuwen (Eds.), Foundations of computer science. Vol. III, part 2: Language, logic, semantics. Amsterdam: Mathematisch Centrum, 3-52.

Nix, D. (1978). Project straight-talk. In Annual meeting of ADCIS. Association for the Development of Computer-Based Instructional Systems.

Nix, R. (1981). Experience with a space efficient way to store a dictionary. Communications of the ACM, 24.
[Dictionary]

Nold, E. W. (1975). Fear and trembling: The humanist approaches the computer. College Composition and Communication, 26(3), 269-73.

> A miniature classic. Nold debunks with intelligence and skill the myths many humanists still have about computers leading to passive, uncreative, apathetic human beings. She calls for a movement away from unimaginative drill and practice programs to more creative forms of computer interaction. A poetry generating program, using sensory questions as prompts, is given as an example of a method of teaching about concrete and abstract ideas. The program is written in what she calls "discovery and surprise" mode. An invention dialogue similar to that of Burns, above, but less complex, is also given as an example. The final example shows how interactive computers can be used to teach concepts such as logical fallacies. It would be interesting to know how some of these programs work--i.e., how they deal with the apparently permissible varied syntactic forms student answers come in (e.g., "No;" "I don't think so;" "Not really") as well as what type of computer (probably a mainframe) the programs run on.
> [Drill and Practice, Poetry Writing, Invention]

Oakman, R. (1980). Computer methods for literary research. Columbia: University of South Carolina Press.

> A good introduction and survey with focus on literary study. See also Hockey.
> [Literary Analysis]

Oates, W. (1981). An evaluation of computer–assisted instruction for English grammar review. In Studies in Language Learning, 3. 193–200. Special issue on "The Plato system and language study," ed. R. S. Hart. (ERIC Document Reproduction Service No. ED 218 930)

Based on use of PLATO's grammar CAI to supplement journalism classes at Indiana University.
[PLATO, Journalism, Computer Aided Instruction]

O'Donnell, H. (1982). Computer literacy, part I: An overview, and Computer literacy, part II: Classroom applications. The Reading Teacher, Jan., 1982, 490–4 and Feb., 1982, 614–7.

Quick view of the major issues with cross references to other lists. Part II contrasts computer-assisted instruction (CAI) with direct learner interaction and dialogue, with computer-managed instruction (CMI) with a major emphasis on record-keeping and test-scoring.
[Computer Literacy, Computer Aided Instruction]

O'Haire, W. W. (1983). The effects of word processing on writing. Unpublished manuscript available from the author, Holy Cross College, Worcester, MA.

A review of rationales for computers and writing precedes the results of a survey conducted to determine undergraduates' reactions to word processing. They were positive, and students claimed that they did more revising and editing with computers than with "regular" methods.
[Testimonial]

Oren, S. S. (1975). A mathematical theory of man–machine document assembly. IEEE Transactions on Systems, Man and Cybernetics, SMC–S 256–67.

Ornstein, J., et al. (1971). Programmed instruction and educational technology in the language teaching field: New approaches to old problems. Language and the teacher: A series in applied linguistics, 9. Center for Curriculum Development, Inc., 401 Walnut St., Philadelphia, PA 19106.

Overfield, K. G. (1980). The effects of a model office simulation on student attitudes toward work, interpersonal relations and knowledge of word-processing principles and concepts. Dissertation Abstracts International, 41(1), 74–A, 75–A.

Overfield attempts to determine if simulation in word–processing instruction is effective in achieving differences in student behaviors and attitudes toward work, interpersonal relations, and word-processing principles. Her prime question: could students apply concepts and principles, taught in a very structured classroom, to a realistic office environment established within the classroom? She found only one

difference between the two groups: knowledge of word-processing concepts and principles. Students in the simulation performed better. No difference was seen in attitudes toward work or interpersonal relations.
[Office of Future]

Packert-Hall, M. & Burke., R. C. (1981). An index to PLATO lessons on composition. No longer available from The Language Learning Laboratory, The University of Illinois, Urbana, IL. Instead, contact one of the authors.

A complete guide to what you can do if you have access to PLATO. Lessons designed for programmed self-instruction. Traditional CAI, not word processing. Categorized to make it easy for instructors following a "diagnosis and prescription" model to find what students should review in PLATO's skills packages. Useful for remediation, writing labs, etc., if one agrees that this is what basic students need.
[PLATO]

Page, E. B. (1966). Grading essays by computer: Progress report. In Proceedings of the 1966 Invitational Conference on Testing Problems, 87-100. Educational Testing Service, Princeton, NJ.
[Evaluation of Writing]

Page, E. B. (1968). The use of the computer in analyzing student essays. International Review of Education, 14, 210-225.
[Evaluation of Writing]

Page, E. B., & Paulus, D. H. (1968). The analysis of essays by computer. (Final report., BR-6-1318) Connecticut University, Storrs. Office of Education (DHEW), Washington, DC. Bureau of Research. (ERIC Document Reproduction Service No. ED 028 633)

Too old, technologically at least, and for many in terms of composition theory as well. Uses keypunch. Concentrates on automatic evaluation of final written product, not on using the computer to help teach writing skills. The subjects of the study are secondary students and the computer ended up picking out the "expert" writers just as "accurately" as human judges. Recommendations for future research are given.
[Evaluation of Writing]

Pask, G. (1982). SAKI: Twenty-five years of adaptive training into the microprocessor era. International Journal of Man-Machine Studies, 17(1), 69-74.

SAKI, a trainer for developing keyboard skills, was first implemented in 1956. Pask traces its development to its current implementation on a microprocessor.
[Human Factors]

Patton, P. C., & Holoien, R. A. (1981). Computing in the humanities. Lexington, MA: D. C. Heath.

Describes 25 ongoing projects at the University of Minnesota.
[Literary Analysis]

Paul, T. & Payne, D. (1978). Computer-assisted instruction: Teaching and learning from basic writers. The Writing Instructor, 2(4) 59-66.

Describes a computer program (SPELLWELL) at Iowa State University which helps students correct their spelling and also gathers data on students' error patterns. As the project advances, the error-rate information will be used to tailor the lessons to students' needs or abilities.
[Spelling checkers]

Payne, D. (1983). Integrating computer-assisted instruction into a writing center. Unpublished paper presented at the Writing Centers Associations Fifth Annual Conference, Purdue University. Available from the author at Iowa State University, Ames.
[Computer Aided Instruction]

Peacock, J., et al. (1977). Information processing and the office of tomorrow. Waltham, MA: International Data Corporation.

Report focuses on hardware, with some notes on how various machines will save money (e.g., by replacing secretaries). It's interesting, also, because lots of the predictions about cost and hardware trends are wrong--costs are lower and machines are better.
[Survey of Hardware, Office of Future]

Pepinsky, H. B. (1978). A computer-assisted language analysis system (CALAS) and its applications. Technical Report, The Ohio State University. (ERIC Document Reproduction Service No. ED 162 663)

This is a project by psychologists--its relevance to writing instruction isn't completely clear--interesting project, though. See Rush, et al., below, for another report.
[Semantics]

Petersen, B. T., Selfe, C. L., & Wahlstrom, B. J. (no date). Computer-assisted instruction and the writing process: 'Well, it looks good, but can it. . .?' Unpublished manuscript available from the authors at Michigan Technological University, Houghton, MI.

Outlines the essential goals of CAI that will teach composing processes and lists

relevant research questions. Appropriate CAI must (1) address significant writing problems, (2) have true process orientation, and suggest the whole process, (3) be rhetorically specific in terms of aim and mode, (4) make students write, rather than do something else, (5) account for the wide range of skills and abilities we know students have, (6) include both writing and computer specialists in its design, and (7) be field-tested before being ready for distribution. The research questions can only begin to be answered after pilot CAI materials are distributed. The questions are whether the CAI (1) guides students through the composing process, (2) supplements classroom instruction, (3) is an alternative to tutors, (4) improves students' attitudes toward writing, (5) is more effective then other ways to teach, and (6) will encourage students to write more.
[Design of Software, Computer Aided Instruction]

Peterson, J. L. (1980). Computer programs for detecting and correcting spelling errors. Communications of the ACM, 23, 676-87.

A good introduction to the theory and types of programs which identify misspelled words. Peterson divides existing spelling programs into two categories, those which simply find misspellings (spelling checkers) and those which also use pattern recognition and coding theory to suggest the most probably correct spelling of the word (spelling correctors). Reference is made to four checking/correcting programs: TYPO and SPELL, both on Bell Lab's UNIX system; the SPELL program which operates on the DEC 10 system, and the IBM program now in use at Thomas J. Watson Research Center in Yorktown Heights. The last program is only mentioned briefly. This paper discusses various ways spelling programs work, describing the use of token lists, diagrams and trigrams, and different types and sizes of dictionaries, notably those which use affixes to cut down on size. It outlines the advantages and disadvantages of these different methods and how spelling checkers can be written using existing software technology, then relates how the author and his students went about writing their own spelling checker/corrector program and the problems they encountered therein. The final section speculates on future checking systems applied to everything from grammar to the semantic content of texts.
[Spelling Checkers, WRITER'S WORKBENCH, EPISTLE]

Petrick, S. R. (1976). On natural language based computer systems. IBM Research Development, 20(4), 302-25; also in A. Zampolli (Ed.), (1977). Linguistic Structures Processing. Amsterdam: North-Holland, 313-40.

Useful survey of many question-answering and language processing approaches, illustrating their capabilities. This sort of article shows up clearly the limits of such systems for a plausible analysis or commentary on texts, whether written by students or anyone else.
[Design of Software]

Piper, K. (1983). Word processing in the classroom: Using microcomputer-delivered sentence combining exercises with elementary students. Proceedings of NECC/5, National Educational Computing Conference 1983. Silver Spring, MD: Institute of Electrical and Electronics Engineers Computer Society Press, 18–21.

Reviews studies of sentence combining, then reports on a small study where fifth graders did lessons out of Strong's Sentence–Combining and Paragraph Building (1981) using an off–the–shelf text editor. Students on the computer were more enthusiastic than students working on paper.
[Sentence Combining Exercises]

Pool, I. de S., & Abelson, R. (1961). The Simulatics Project. The Public Opinion Quarterly, 25, 167–183.

Old attempt at computer–based audience analysis, using the results of public opinion polls from the 1960 presidential campaign to project the impact of issues on various audiences of voters. Voter types were reduced to a 480 by 52 matrix based on socio–economic status and campaign issues. The matrix, when accessed, would simulate a given voting block's response to a given issue. Rather limited applicability, but might provide the seeds for an audience analysis heuristic.

Poteet, G. H.. (1968). The computer and the teacher of English. Newark, NJ: New Jersey Association of Teachers of English.

Pournelle, J. (1979). Writing with a microcomputer. onComputing, 1(1), 12–14, 16–19.

Basically an anecdotal account of how one writer came to writing with computers; it is not much use to us. It may be useful, however, to beginning students to see someone go through the trials of learning these beasties.
[Testimonial]

Pournelle, J. (1982). Terminal madness, THE WORD, GRAMMATIK, and then some. BYTE, June 1982, 286–300.

Among other things, Pournelle provides brief commentary on the IBM–PC keyboard (a disappointment, he claims) the Televideo terminal, and various word processing software packages: THE WORD, a spelling checker from Oasis system (he compares it to Spellguard), WRITE from Ashton Tate, a word processing system which he thinks will "blow WORDSTAR out of the market," (p. 296)––not enough information here to assess the truth of that remark––and Aspen Software's PROOFREADER and GRAMMATIK.
[THE WORD, Spelling Checkers, GRAMMATIK]

Powers, R. S. (1981). Computer assisted English instruction. In R. B. Shuman (Ed.), Education in the 80's: English. Washington: National Education Association, 108–112. (ERIC Document Reproduction Service No. ED 199 762)

Competent, if typical, apologetics. Paper begins by dispelling humanist fears, and distinguishing between fact and myth concerning the computer: we don't need to fear being "squeezed out" by one; it can instead be "a drillmaster, an illustrator, and a challenger." Argues that the individualized attention a computer can give a student does not dehumanize that student's education but in fact makes it more humane. Reminds reader that the computer is "patient"; it can deal with mechanics without getting bored or feeling like a drudge, unlike most teachers, and can free teachers themselves to do the really "creative" work. Powers points out the increased feasibility of CAI with the advent of the microprocessor, claiming "it is now economically possible for the average school district to employ full-scale CAI," and advocating a ratio of one terminal for every five or six students. No mention of word processors. Powers is associated with the PLATO project at the University of Illinois.
[Computer Aided Instruction, PLATO]

Press, L. (1980). Word processors: A look at four popular programs. onComputing, 2(1), 38-52.

Summarizes for authors the various options in choosing word-processing programs. He compares AUTO SCRIBE, ELECTRIC PENCIL, MAGIC WAND, and WORDSTAR. Some of his introductory remarks on word processing in general are well-written and could be used to instruct beginning students.
[WORDSTAR]

Preston, J. (1976). A plain man's guide to word processing. Modern Office and Data Management (Australia), 15(11), 4-6.

Price, L. A. (1978). Representing text structure for automatic processing. (Computer Sciences Technical Report #324) Madison, WI: Univ. of Wisconsin.

A sophisticated discourse-linguistics project and proposal--might give some hints about invention programming. This was Price's dissertation.

Price, L. A. (in press). THUMB: An interactive tool for accessing and maintaining text. Institute of Electrical and Electronics Engineers.

Not directly relevant to writing, but contains some interesting information about how a computer program may use treeing as a way of representing hierarchical relationships in text structures. Unlike the work of Stromfors and Jonesjo, below, which relies on treeing as a means of supplying text structure, THUMB uses tree structure to provide readers with a system for locating passages within a text; that is, it is designed merely to recognize existing structure.
[Design of Software]

Prokop, M. (1975). Systematic performance analysis in foreign language instruction.

The Fourth World Conference of the International Association of Applied Linguistics.

Not on English composition, but it treats an important issue.
[ESL]

Quade, B. (1978).   Computer use in education.   Education Update, 12, 67.

Quinones, E. R. (1972).   Programs for developing a document encoding and retrieval system: English text preparation and the analysis of word clusters.   The Consistent System.   (Technical Report 72-1) Cambridge: Cambridge Project.

Riddle, E. A. (1976).   Comparative study of various text editors and formatting systems. (Report No. AD-A029 050) Washington, DC: Air Force Data Services Center/Air Force Automation Agency.
A very useful study, but differences between text processing and word processing become significant at this point; these are "on-line" text editors and formatting systems designed to provide data processing systems with text processing capability; consequently even the simplest system described here is more complicated than most academic writing requires.   The various text processing systems compared have no doubt been substantially modified since 1976; the study's chief importance lies rather in the Summary statement and tables of desirable features for file management, text editor capabilities, and text formatter capabilities which would be quite sound models for further comparative work.   Riddle goes into great detail in specifying features: ability to distinguish between permanent and working copy, retention of several versions of a file concurrently, type of cursor (character or line oriented), modes of address, paragraph recognition, ability to define page size, line length, margins, etc.   At the end of her report is an individual analysis of the strengths and weaknesses of each editing system.   The first section, "Desirable Implementation of Various File Structure, Text Editor and Formatting Functions" is not easy reading, perhaps due to the lack of clear examples of writing/editing situations where these functions are desirable.   It might be better read after the Summary section on page 15, which gives a clearer context for its prescriptions.

Riddle also classifies formatting systems into three types: those which provide a set format by default, with a limited range of alternatives; those which offer different formats according to structure type, but which require the user to implement the formatting commands necessary for that type, and those in which the user defines and executes macros for specific structure types, with the system itself being pre-programmed to supply the necessary commands.   She concludes that the last formatting system is the most desirable, because users can produce final documents from source texts quickest.
[Survey of Software, Typesetting]

Rieger, B. (1979). Linguistic semantics and the problem of vagueness: On analyzing and representing word meaning. In D. E. Ager, F. E. Knowles, & J. Smith (Eds.), Advances in computer-aided literary and linguistic research. Birmingham, UK: Department of Modern Languages, University of Aston, 271-288.
[Semantics]

Riskin, J. (1972). Written composition and the computer. Educational Technology, 12(6), 46-51. (ERIC Document Reproduction Service No. ED 078 678)

> According to Riskin, programmed instruction is little employed as a medium for teaching people to write effectively. Since composition involves the production of original sentences, and current computer facilities are not yet sufficiently powerful to deal with this phenomenon, it is not feasible to have a complete computer-assisted instruction (CAI) writing course. Nevertheless, it is possible to give instruction in many of the basic skills and concepts which precede writing. To accomplish this, a CAI system must have two capabilities, conceptual comparison and phonetic spelling. Given these, it is possible to construct a hierarchy of concepts, for example: audience, purpose, strategy, thesis, research, organization, introduction, transition, conclusion, paragraphs, and sentences. Assuming that the student has skills relevant to each concept, it is possible to develop relevant lessons.
> [Computer Aided Instruction]

Ritchie, D. M., & Thompson, K. (1978). The UNIX time sharing system. Bell Systems Technical Journal (UNIX issue), 57(6), 1905-1929.

> UNIX is a general-purpose, multi-user, interactive operating system which runs on DEC's PDP-11 and the Interdata 8132 computers, among others. This paper discusses the hierarchical file system and the user command interface. The article requires an intermediate level of technical expertise.
> [Design of Software, UNIX]

Roberts, T. L. & Moran, T. P. (1982). Evaluation of text editors. In Eight short papers in user psychology, T. P. Moran. (Ed.), Palo Alto, CA: Xerox PARC, 5-10.

> Technical evaluation is presented as a research methodology. Subjects were given a set of editing and formatting tasks to do on fixed texts and then evaluated in terms of execution time, errors, and learning. Eight editing systems were evaluated with these results: (1) CRT-based systems were faster than print-based ones, (2) users' errors were more variable than system errors, (3) different systems had a wide range of learning times; however, speed of learning and speed of expert use correlate positively (they are not traded off). Some general conclusions: (1) it would take an experienced evaluator about a week to check out a new editor, (2) experts take about 30 seconds to perform a typical task, (3) it takes about two hours of one-on-one training to get new users familiar with the core tasks of most editing systems, (4) slower users make more errors, and (5)

novice and expert users have about the same range of variation.
[Human Factors]

Robey, D., & Taggart, W. (1982). Human information processing in information and decision support systems. Management Information Systems Quarterly, 6(2), 61-73.

Explores the relevance of human brain structure to the development and use of a computer-based information and decision support system. The electronic computer performs only logical, sequential operations, and is, in a sense, a model of the left brain and not the right. Three implications emerge from this classification. First, research using cognitive style to predict decision behavior should include intuitive as well as analytical styles, even though intuition cannot be modeled in the traditional sense. Second, this article suggests a division of labor between the computer and the human for various types of decision making. Third, information systems should support the type of processing required by the task, including both right and left hemisphere processes.
[Human Factors]

Robinson, P., & Singer, D. (1981). Another spelling correction program. Communications of the ACM, 24(5).
[Spelling Checkers]

Roblyer, M. D. (1981). Instructional design versus authoring of courseware: Some crucial differences. AEDS Journal, 14, 173-81.

Discusses important distinctions between instructional design, a term coined by learning theorists and military/industrial trainers to describe a model-based, systems approach to creating effective instruction for various technologies, and authoring, a term adopted by developers during the early part of the microcomputer boom to describe a more generic development process. Describes a courseware design model and systematic procedures to assure that courseware facilitates student learning.
[Authoring System, Design of Software]

Roch, B. (1980). More mileage from your text editor. Interface Age, 5(2), 83-87.
[Testimonial]

Rohlfs, S. (1979). User interface requirements. Convergence, Infotech State of the Art Report, 2, Maidenhead, England, 165-199.

Roman, R. (1978). Machines need people. Word Processing Now (Great Britain), November 1978, 16-17, 20, 22-3.

This is an office study on how to obtain, train, and retain word processing staff.

It's somewhat dated, but it might be useful to anyone interested in promoting good interaction between students and machines.
[Human Factors, Office of Future]

Roman, D. (1981). The case for specialized word processors. Computer Decisions, 13(6), 60-2, 64, 70, 72.

Rosenberg, S. (1977). Frames-based text processing. (MIT Artificial Intelligence Memo #431.) (NTIS number AD-A052-444).
[Semantics]

Ross, D. (1973). Beyond the concordance: Algorithms for description of English clauses and phrases. In A. J. Aitken, R. W. Bailey, & N. Hamilton-Smith (Eds.), The computer and literary studies. Edinburgh: Edinburgh University Press, 85-99.

Only valuable for people who need to write programs which will do surface-structure syntactic analysis; describes a slot-and-filler procedure which is based on a function-word dictionary. Related to the EYEBALL programs developed by Ross and Rasche.
[EYEBALL]

Rothkopf, E. Z., & Johnson, P. E. (Eds.). (1971). Verbal learning research and the technology of written instruction. New York: Teachers College Press, Columbia University.

Not relevant. The "technology of written instruction" refers to any technical medium used to produce written language, the purpose of which is to teach (outside of mere handwriting). It does not mean computer-aided writing instruction. One paper, by Max V. Matthews of Bell Labs, entitled "The computer in the technology of written instruction," is mainly concerned with how computers can aid in the publication of instructional material (editing, formatting, etc). The symposium was some time ago (1966), and the discussion is necessarily dated.

Rothmann, M. A. (1980). The writer's craft transformed: Word processing. onComputing, 2(3), 60-62.

Essentially a testimonial to word processing for writers. May be useful as an offering to beginning students.
[Testimonial]

Rouse, W. B. (1975). Design of man-computer interfaces for on-line interactive systems. Proceedings of the IEEE, 63, 847-857.
[Human Factors]

RSVP: Feedback program for individualized analysis of writing. Manual for faculty
users, part 1: Analyzing students' writing (1979). New York: Exxon Education
Foundation. See Anandam, et al., and Kotler, above. (ERIC Document Reproduction
Service No. ED 190 167)

A manual for and introduction to the Response System with Variable Prescription
(RSVP) program, which produces individualized letters to reinforce student
learning and help correct writing errors. After reviewing RSVP's history, this
report describes in detail the four levels of commentary provided by the system:
basic (A), intermediate (B), and superior (C) levels, which provide corrective
prescriptions for 156 mechanical and rhetorical errors, and a level (P) which gives
out non-prescriptive explanations of such fundamentals as sentence structure, verb
tense, and pronoun usage. Examples of RSVP's letters follow--welcome letters,
assignment feedback letters, status reports, and final reports--as well as guidelines
for how to assign appropriate levels of commentary to each student. Examples of
student essays representing each level are also included, with an illustration of an
appropriately marked computer card, and a sample feedback letter for that
student.
[Evaluation of Writing, RSVP]

Rubin, A. (1980). Making stories, making sense. Language Arts, 280-298.

Interesting to read after "The computer confronts language arts," below, since this
describes STORY MAKER and its accompanying activities primarily as they existed
without the computer--via peg or bulletin boards, index card "nodes" and yarn
"branches." The editing and revision of stories was accomplished by switching
index cards. A brief description of the experimental computer version is given.
What's important to note is that many of the goals STORY MAKER has as a
computer program can also be accomplished effectively without computer
mediation: the ability to bring students together for writing tasks, free them
from attending to low-level details such as grammar and spelling to concentrate
on more global writing issues, and give them opportunities to see each other's
work something unique to the computer. If not, what are the advantages to
implementing these goals on a computer, the rationale behind using the computer
to accomplish these goals? The difference between STORY MAKER as a
classroom activity and STORY MAKER as a computer activity in this version is
that the tree structure itself is not displayed--students must select alternatives
without the visual aid of following a "path." Later versions of STORY MAKER
incorporate a window which displays the tree. The other major difference is the
printout, the effects of which are also discussed in Zaccher, below.
[STORY MAKER, Elementary Writing]

Rubin, A. (1982). The computer confronts language arts: Cans and shoulds for
education. In A.C. Wilkinson (Ed.), Classroom computers and cognitive science. New
York: Academic Press.

Directed mainly toward teachers of younger writers, but contains some useful points about directions for microcomputers and writing. Rubin, operating out of the research group at Bolt Beranek and Newman, Inc., challenges traditional perspectives on computers as instructional tools primarily for drill and classroom management. "Given the overwhelming presence of programs that dwell on letters, words and sentences," she asserts, "designers of educational software should make programs with a more sophisticated view of language a high priority," She also makes a useful distinction between response and feedback. A computer can give a "blind" response, but feedback about a student's text itself is a stickier subject when one gets beyond what programs like those in WRITER'S WORKBENCH (see Frase et al.) can do.

The STORY MAKER program developed by Bolt Beranek and Newman, which runs on an Apple II, has probably the most potential as a prototype for college level "treeing" exercises. It helps teach students about overall features of a text--coherence, logical flow, the place of details and examples, etc.--rather than concentrating merely on the word or sentence level. STORY MAKER uses a tree structure to allow children to create stories by choosing options from a set of pre-written story segments. At the beginning of a student's session, a statement of the story's basic goal, something like a statement of purpose, is selected. On one part of the screen, the story tree itself is displayed, and students can see their progress down the tree, at least on a color screen, because their choices appear in a different color. A second program, STORY MAKER, allows students to add their own segments to the story tree.

The other program discussed here, TEXTMAN, is an electronic Hangman game in which parts of already written texts must be put in the appropriate order by students. The purpose is to teach something about the chronological and sequential constraints of a text, and about the logic of transitions. Author, intended audience, and purpose may be specified; student may also see the immediate context of the text they're ordering--a few paragraphs which precede and/or follow the text in question.

What she has found about language arts programs for young children is analogous to the state of affairs in programs for college writers. Of 105 she and her group examined, 9 required letter-level tinkering, 85 involved word level choices, 7 played around with phrases or sentences. Only 7 had anything resembling whole texts for students to read or respond to.

The article goes on to suggest the need to explore alternatives to Yes/No computer feedback--e.g., students responding to one another via the computer--and discusses the advantages of text editors for elementary students, much of which is applicable to any writer. Potential uses for formatting options and for message systems (electronic mail) are also discussed.
[Design of Software, Elementary Writing, STORY MAKER]

Rubin, A. D., & Gentner, D. (1979). An education technique to encourage practice with high-level aspects of text. Paper presented at the National Reading Conference.

Reprints available from the author, Bolt Beranek and Newman, Inc., 50 Moulton Street, Cambridge, MA 02238.

Rubinstein, R., & Goldberg, P. (1978). Using a computer message system for promoting reading and writing in a school for the deaf. Proceedings of the Fifth Annual Conference on Systems for the Disabled, Houston, TX.
[Handicapped Persons]

Rude, R. V., Malone, D. L., & Mooers, C. D. (1979). The Hermes Message System. Cambridge, MA: Bolt Beranek and Newman, Inc. Copies are available from Bolt Beranek and Newman Inc., 50 Moulton Street, Cambridge, MA 02238.
[Communication Systems]

Rudisill, V. (1983). The San Antonio College English multimedia laboratory: Variations on traditional instructional time. Unpublished paper presented at the Writing Centers Association Fifth Annual Conference. Available from the author at San Antonio College.

Rudisill, V. A., & Jabs, M. L. (1976). Multimedia instruction in basic English. San Antonio, TX. (ERIC Document Reproduction Service No. ED 128 056)

CAI for basic language skills—drill and practice, tutorial. Project is directed toward freshmen at San Antonio who need individualized help. Other media--tapes, slides, etc.--are also employed.
[Computer Aided Instruction]

Rudisill, V. A., & Jabs, Max L. (1977). Multimedia for reading & writing. Community & Junior College Journal 47(8), 16-18. (ERIC Document Reproduction Service No. EJ 160 792)

Shorter version of Rudisill & Jabs, above.

Rush, J. E., Pepinsky, H. B., Meara, N. M., Landy, B. C., Strong, S. M., Valley, J. A., & Young, C. E. (1974). A computer-assisted language analysis system. (Technical Report, Computer and Information Science Research Center) Columbus, OH: The Ohio State University.

See Pepinsky, above.
[Semantics]

Russ-Eft, D. F, McLaughlin, D. H., & Elman, A. (1983). Issues for the development of reading and writing software. Palo Alto, CA: American Institutes for Research in the Behavioral Sciences. Available from AIR, P. O. Box 1113, Palo Alto, CA. 94302.

A general introduction to basic research on reading and writing skills which lend themselves to CAI, with a discussion of the economic and professional incentives which teachers and researchers in these fields will have to have to begin to produce quality software in their disciplines.
[Computer Aided Instruction]

Sallis, P. H. (1978). A partial-parsing algorithm for natural language text using a simple grammar for arguments. Association for Literary and Linguistic Computing Bulletin, 6(2), 170-176.

Proposes a production chain that describes the contents of empirical arguments in scientific text. Parsing rules, using this chain as a grammar, yield a structure of the argument in terms of probabalistic and deterministic approaches to text analysis. Finally an algorithm is given which incorporates the approaches with the grammar and the rules.
[Design of Software, Syntax]

Sallis, P. H. (1978). Concept parsing rules for generating an information structure from natural language text. Journal of Informatics, 2(2), 107-116.

Describes progress toward implementing a computer model for analyzing text to produce an information structure. A three-part rule is proposed for analyzing a text. The process of information transfer and the synthesis of information from the text with a subject state-of-knowledge is discussed in terms of the rationale for choosing this structure.
[Syntax]

Samet, H. (1982). Heuristics for the line division problem in computer justified text. Communications of the ACM, 25, 564-71.

Argues that documents are more visually pleasing with the deviations in spaces between words reduced, and suggests measures for evaluating solutions to the line division problem; technical.
[Typesetting]

Sanford, D. & Roach, J. W. (1982). Evaluating natural language communication to improve human-computer interaction. IEEE, 194-98.

Small-scale study of whether naive users learn a computing task better if the input is in natural language or a restricted command language. People adapt about as well to either situation rather quickly.
[Human Factors]

School's word processing students much in demand. (1980). The Office, 92(3), 158, 160.

Briefly sketches the word-processing program at Shawsheen Valley Technical High School. Mostly a discussion of the program and the school, but does give some specifics of the instruction: students check hard copy for accuracy and completeness and then make the corrections on the screen; students receive basic instruction [not specified], and students find that much of their learning is achieved by practice, comparing experiences, and sharing knowledge. No data are given on the effectiveness of this program, except to say that all the school's students who graduate find jobs, but this may be due more to a high demand for operators and a low supply of them.
[Secondary Writing]

Schrodt, P. (1982). The generic word processor: A word-processing system for all your needs. BYTE, 7:4, 32, 34, 36.

Account of the wonders of pencil-and-paper and scissors-and-paste procedures, old style. A mock-technical report, with no comments on writing theory. Comic relief.
[Primitive Systems]

Schuelbe, D., & King, D. T. (1983). New technology in the classroom: Computers and communication and the future. T. H. E. Journal, 10(6), 95-100.

Reviews computer-assisted instruction in various areas related to writing instruction, computer conferences, and data bases. Ends with a list of "commercially available online data bases" available through Lockeed or Bibliographical Retrieval Service as of October 1980.
[Computer Aided Instruction, Data Bases]

Schuyler, J. A. (1979). Programming languages for microprocessor courseware. Educational Technology, 19(10), 29-35.

A very good, clear introduction to programming languages, specifically regarding their advantages and disadvantages for authoring courseware. The author explains the differences between the general programming languages BASIC and PASCAL, and also discusses PILOT (from Western Washington University) and TUTOR (from Control Data), both of which are designed specifically as problem-oriented languages for courseware authors. Pros and cons of using direct coding versus a driver program, and compilers versus interpreters, are also discussed. Authoring systems and what they do wraps up this introduction. Tables and diagrams are provided, and these contribute to the article's clarity.
[Design of Software, Authoring System]

Schwartz, H. J. (1981). Teaching stylistic simplicity with a computerized readability formula. Paper presented at the International Conference of the American Business Communication Association, Washington, DC, December 1980. (ERIC Document

Reproduction Service No. ED 196 014)

A study to assess whether readability formulas can really help students in business and technical writing classes write with the stylistic simplicity appropriate to their audience and purpose. Two classes of each were studied, one of which got feedback on their writing from General Motors' STAR, a readability test based on the Flesch Index, the other of which was a control group. Five assignments were tested; a nine-point scale determined appropriateness of stylistic simplicity. The results, while not conclusive, suggested that readability feedback may increase the correlation of overall achievement to stylistic simplicity. The overall achievement of students in the STAR group correlated more positively with scores on the stylistic simplicity scale than did overall achievement of control group students. The control group scores on the stylistic simplicity scale did not predict overall achievement: these students could apparently learn how to achieve simpler style, but their learning did not consistently lead to improved overall writing.
[Readability]

Schwartz, H. J. (1981). Keeping CAI humane in the humanities. National Computer Conference Proceedings, 50, 605-8.

A version of "Monsters and Mentors," below; reviews typical CAI programs to show what kinds of applications exist in the humanities, and critiques them.
[Computer Aided Instruction]

Schwartz, H. J. (1982). A computer program for invention and audience feedback. Paper presented at the Conference on College Composition and Communication, San Francisco. Available from the author, Department of English, Oakland University, Rochester, MI.

A report of an attempt to test a program to aid students in literature classes (college level) by teaching them a heuristic for invention as they investigated characters in works they read. Innovative in that students not only wrote with the system, but were able to share their writing with peers and with the instructor through a network which gave others access to what was written and the ability to comment on that writing. While her results did not show an improvement in writing quality (essay exams), this is definitely the kind of imaginative programming we should see more of if we are to tap the potential of the computer for interacting with the writing process.
[Evaluation of Writing, Literary Analysis]

Schwartz, H. J. (1982). Monsters and mentors: Computer applications for humanistic education. College English, 44(2), 141-152.

While this doesn't discuss word processing, it's a good summary of just about everything else that's going on which relates computer programs with writing. Schwartz divides available computer applications into 4 areas: text feedback, drill and practice, simulations (especially those dealing with poetry) and tutorials, and

shows how each is presently being used. (Hugh Burns's work is cited as a tutorial application.) Her references are particularly helpful; even those which seem tangential have been incorporated in this bibliography. Schwartz concludes with a section on "choosing, using and developing computer programs" which poses good questions for those interested in how word processors and their software can best serve the needs of student writers.
[INVENT, Survey of Software]

Schwartz, H. J. (1983). Computer aids to individualized instruction throughout the writing process. Unpublished manuscript, available from the author, Oakland University, Rochester, MI.

Ideas for using CAI and word processing with existing programs.
[Computer Aided Instruction]

Schwartz, H. J. (1983). A computer program for active learning in literary criticism. Unpublished manuscript.

Describes in detail Schwartz's interactive programs for writing about literature, MARSY (Mentor and Recording Secretary) and EBB (Electronic Bulletin Board). Also the reports on results of using these programs with 38 students for nine weeks. Schwartz claims these programs are successful because they allow for non-judgmental tutorials--at a time and place comfortable for the student and because the computer medium makes it possible for students to "talk" to each other about their writing, via the electronic bulletin board, in a non-threatening environment that fosters critical thinking and audience awareness. The program can be easily adapted to other content.
[Literary Analysis]

Schwartz, H. J., & Bridwell, L. S. (in press). Selected bibliography on computers in composition. College Composition and Communication.

A brief survey of the publications the compilers believed to be most immediately helpful for college writing teachers.
[Bibliography]

Schwartz, M. (1982). Computers and the teaching of writing. Educational Technology, 22, 27-29.

Science (1982) 215(4534), special issue on "Computers and Electronics" and Scientific American (September 1977) (since published as a W. H. Freeman book), special issue on "microelectronics."

Both of these special issues give excellent surveys of current and forthcoming technical advances. Articles in both are clearly written--probably the best

background reading you can get.
[Survey of Software, Survey of Hardware, Communication Systems, Data Bases]

Scowen, R. S. (1981). A survey of some text editors. Software--Practice and Experience, 11(9), 883-905.

>Reviews several editors and discusses the tasks they perform, constraints on them, and their user interfaces. Includes a glossary of terms.
>[Survey of Software, Glossary]

Scrizzi, A., & Ung, V. (1975). The teaching of typewriting: An application of microprocessors. Amsterdam, Netherlands: North-Holland, 171-175.

>Describes a new application of microprocessors: The design of an autonomous station for the teaching of typewriting. Several European researchers have become involved in keyboard design. This may be an area to watch for developments.
>[Human Factors]

Selfe, C., & Wahlstrom, B.J. (1983). The benevolent beast: Computer assisted instruction for the teaching of writing. The Writing Instructor, 2, 183-192.

>Descriptions of an interactive program, WORDSWORTH II, with planning and polishing modules for different assignments (narration, evaluation, persuasion, etc.).
>[WORDSWORTH II, Computer Aided Instruction]

Serafini, M. T. (1982). Methodology for planning curricula in teaching writing. Unpublished manuscript, available from the author, Istituto di Cibernetica, Univ. di Milano, I-20133, Milano, Italy.

>Serafini sees a writing curriculum as a progression through various genres or modes, from simple description to jokes. Certain "base skills," e.g., gathering evidence, determining cause-effect relationships, are seen as being especially important for some formats. In a final, brief paragraph she proposes a computer program that will "include in the curriculum those writing modes which are specified by the teacher" for the individual student.

Serwer, B. L., & Stolurow, L. M. (1970). CAI learning in language arts. Elementary English, 47(5), 641-650.

>Not useful.
>[Computer Aided Instruction]

Sharma, D. K., & Gruchacz, A. M. (1982). The display text editor TED: A case study in the design and implementation of display-oriented interactive human interfaces.

IEEE Transactions on Communications, 30.

What is most useful here, if you're not interested directly in TED (an overview of which is provided along with an evaluation and a description of its architecture) is the section on design criteria. The authors discuss how TED was designed to ensure ease of learning, remembering, and use, as well as safety and customizability. Learning is facilitated by a graded command structure and by making certain functions of the editor (tabs, margins, etc.) similar in appearance and operation to those of a typewriter. Moreover, a synonym facility is provided, allowing more experienced users to change command names to those they are familiar with from other editing systems. Remembering is made easier by a consistent command structure, by mnemonics, and by distinct command names. In the section discussing ease of use, the issue of power vs. simplicity is addressed, as well as criteria for useful feedback, the need for an unobstrusive editor, and the means by which TED prevents unnecessary typing. How well this all worked, and how quickly a user can move up the ladder is described in the evaluation section: seven secretaries, none of whom had used a screen-oriented editor before, and several who had never used a terminal, learned the elementary commands in less than 30 minutes. The safety section discusses accidental insertion and deletion; customizability issues addressed include setting parameters, renaming commands, and creating new commands.
[Design of Software, Human Factors]

Sharples, M. (1980). A computer based language workshop. ACM SIGCUE Bulletin, 14(3), 7-17. Condensed from Department of Artificial Intelligence Research Paper Nos. 134 (9 pages), and 135 (11 pages), 1980. Forest Hill, Edinburgh EH1 2QL Scotland: Department of Artificial Intelligence, University of Edinburgh.

Describes a pilot study language workshop which provided children with a small range of language manipulation tools to bring out a child's intuitive understanding of language and widen her creative writing skills. The workshop concentrates on style, not correctness. The natural language computer program in use here allows students to generate sentences from a grammar, add constraints of syntax and semantics, and discover how simple transformation rules work. The object is to allow a student to play with language and thus to explore its potential. The second phase of the project will concentrate more on written style and have a wider range of manipulative capabilities.
[Elementary Writing, Semantics]

Sharples, M. (1981). A computer-based teaching scheme for creative writing. In B. Lewis & D. Tagg (Eds.), Computers in Education: Proceedings of the IFIP (International Federation for Information Processing) TC-3 & 3rd World Conference on Computers in Education. North-Holland, Amsterdam: IFIP, 483-488.
[Poetry Writing]

Shaw, M. L. G. (1982). Tracking the creativity cycle with a microcomputer.

International Journal of Man-Machine Studies, 17(1), 75-85.

A major attraction of introducing electronic technology in education has been individualized instruction. However, it is difficult to a represent each student's prior knowledge. Kelly's personal construct psychology is presented as one framework for the analysis of the learning process, particularly for the practical determination of relevant features of the student's prior knowledge. His notions of constructive and creativity cycles in particular, are of major theoretical significance, can be studied through interactive programs.

Sheridan, T. B., & Ferrell, W. R. (1974). Man-machine systems: Information, control, and decision models of human performance. Cambridge, MA: MIT Press.

Shneiderman, B. (1979). Human factors in designing interactive systems. Computer, 12, 9-19.
[Human Factors]

Shneiderman, B. (1980). Software Psychology. Cambridge, MA: Winthrop.
[Human Factors]

Shostak, R. (1981). Computers and teaching English: Bits 'n' pieces. The Computing Teacher, 9(3), 49-51.

A "commercial" for Hugh Burns' invention programming (see reviews of his work). Gives a sample of the kind of dialogue which occurs between the student and the computer.
[INVENT]

Shostak, R. (1982). Computer-assisted composition instruction: the state of the art. In J. Lawlor (Ed.). Computers in composition instruction. Los Alamitos, CA: SWRL Educational Research and Development.

Provides a good overview of some important programs but the level of writer he's discussing is a little unclear; the paper seems to refer to elementary and secondary students, but with the exception of Andee Rubin's STORY MAKER, all the programs described are designed for college level students or nonacademic writers (e.g., WRITER'S WORKBENCH). Programs reviewed, in addition to those two, include Hugh Burns's invention program, Stephen Marcus's COMPUPOEM, Edmund Skellings' THE ELECTRIC POET, Robert Wisher's Navy programs and Kamala Anandam's RSVP. A brief section on word processors is introductory and contains no references. There is a short mention of the SWRL project, and a smart definition of what "state of the art" should mean for computer instruction.
[WRITER'S WORKBENCH, INVENT, COMPUPOEM, RSVP, STORY MAKER]

Shostak, R. (1983). Computer-assisted instruction: Some promising practices. Pipeline, 8(1), 4-6.

A brief review of promising programs or research around the country; the relevant ones are annotated elsewhere in this bibliography (see Bolt, Beranek & Newman, H. Burns, Marcus, Anandam, Lawlor, WRITER'S WORKBENCH).

Simmons, R. F., & Chester, D. (1982). Relating sentences and semantic networks with procedural logic. Communications of the ACM, 25(8), 527-47.

A system of symmetrical, clausal-logic axioms can transform a thirteen-sentence narrative about a V-2 rocket flight into semantic case relations. The same axioms translate the case relations into English sentences. An approach to defining schemas in the clausal logic is applied in the form of a schema to compute a partitioning of the semantic network. Properties of rule symmetry and network compression are important for natural language processing. Because of the conciseness of the logic interpreter and the clausal representation for grammars and schemas, the procedural logic approach provides a programming system that is promising for natural language analysis on mini- and microcomputers as well as on large mainframes.
[Semantics]

Simms, J. (1982). Evaluating word processors--keyboards: Vital features. Modern Office and Data Management, 21(6), 28-30.

Discusses detached, hence movable keyboards, physical size, systems which allow interchangeable keyboards, and software programming of keyboard keys which allows a trained typist to increase words-per-minute substantially.
[Human Factors]

Sinnott, L. T. (1976). Generative computer-assisted instruction and artificial intelligence. Princeton, NJ: Educational Testing Service.

Slack, J. D. (1982). Assessing the role of the computer in technical and professional communications. Paper presented at the College Composition and Communication Convention, San Francisco.

A timely, "philosophical" warning about the potential misuses of computers in technical writing. Not only is Slack worried about the kind of formulaic, slot-filler writing which can result from simple-minded applications of computers to the writing process, but she is also concerned about the effects of this kind of pseudo-writing within organizations where the flow of information can be tightly controlled by restricting the formats for communication via computers.

Slotnick, H. B. (1972) Toward a theory of computer essay grading. Journal of

Educational Measurement, 9(4), 253-263.

> Too old to be useful, other than as history.
> [Evaluation of Writing]

Smith, A. (1980). Goodbye, Guttenberg: The newspaper revolution of the 1980's. New York: Oxford University Press.

> Not very technical discussion of the economic and social effects of computers (in general) on the newspaper business, including VDTs (video display terminals) for writers and editors. Information flow is touched on, but writing issues are not. The first working programs did "h-and-j" (hyphenation and justification) which went into service about 1962; full page mark up (to avoid pasting) was about a decade later.
> [Journalism]

Smith, J. B. (1976). Encoding literary texts: Some considerations. Association of Literary and Linguistic Computing Bulletin, 4(3), 190-6.

> Attempts to locate a range of problems that a researcher is likely to face when entering a text into a computer system. Not directly relevant.

Smith, W. H. and Pearson, O. R. (1982-83). GRAMR1: A computer program for instruction in formal syntax. Journal of Educational Technology Systems. 11, 167-184.

> For formal linguistics courses, a simple program to test the grammaticality of sentences. The syntax is a very small subset of English, and the lexicon quite limited. Other programs in the GRAMR series are developed, but none will allow for unrestricted English texts.
> [Syntax]

Sneeringer, J. (1978). User-interface design for text editing: A case study. Software--Practice and Experience (Great Britain), 8(5), 53-57.

> An attempt to formulate principles for designing user interfaces, using a text editor named Occam as an example, to illustrate the following considerations: the editor's powerfulness vs. its ease of learning, how prototypes and user feedback may be employed, the importance of planning, and detecting and handling errors. May have implications for powerful word processing programs that are difficult to learn.
> [Human Factors]

Sokoloff, M. (1982). Word processors: A look at five options. Media and Methods, 18.

> [Survey]

Southwell, M. G. (no date) The value of computer-assisted instruction in developmental writing. Available from the author: Department of English, York College/CUNY, Jamaica, NY, 11451.

A rationale for beginning with the obvious with computers: what Southwell calls "closed-ended" programs, i.e., those with "right and wrong" answers to exercises on writing conventions and grammatical forms. Not a bad rationale for a limitation on the use of computers in writing, but one that we do not accept. If one buys his limitation, the paper has 7 useful prescriptions for developing software.
[Design of Software, Computer Aided Instruction]

Southwell, M. G. (1982). Computers and developmental writing at York College/CUNY. The Computing Teacher, 10, 34-35.

An attempt to integrate drill-learned grammar into remedial writing practice.
[Grammar Drill]

Southwell, M. (1982). Computers and developmental writing. The Computing Teacher.

Describes exercises on grammatical and syntactic problems, called the "COMP-LAB Exercises." Information is available from Prentice-Hall, 200 Old Tappan Road, Old Tappan, NJ 07675.
[Grammar Drill]

Southwell, M. G. (1982). Using computer-assisted instruction for developmental writing. AEDS Bulletin, 15, 80-91.

Southwell, M. G. (1983). Computer-assisted instruction in composition at York College/CUNY: Grammar for basic writing students. The Writing Instructor, 2, 165-173.

A longer version of the brief announcements in other journals.

Southwell, M. G. (1983). Using computers for developmental writing instruction. Pipeline, 8(1), 13-16.

Examples of Southwell's interactive grammar programming.
[Grammar Drill]

Southwell, M. G. (in press). Computer-assisted instruction in the COMP-LAB at York College/CUNY. The Writing Lab Newsletter.

Southwell, M. G. (in press). Using computers in teaching reasoning and writing.

Collegiate Microcomputer.

Sparks, M. K. (1978). Help for the harried teacher: A directory of journalistic programmed instruction. In Annual Meeting of the Association for Education in Journalism Association for Education in Journalism.

Spitler, C. D., & Corgan, V. E. (1979). Rules for authoring computer-assisted instruction programs. Educational Technology, 19,(11), 13-20.

> A good introduction to authoring CAI; it provides guidelines for well designed CAI, using English grammar lessons as examples. It is not particularly focused on writing or college students, but there is much of general use. The authors' definition of CAI is a little controversial, in that it rules out drill and practice as genuine computer-aided instruction: "A program is not CAI when it simply consists of a series of drills to which the student responds. True CAI is tutorial." (authors' italics). They also distinguish CAI from CBT, computer-based testing, discuss goals for CAI, and devote a good deal of space to structures and features of good CAI programs. Programming and distribution problems are also treated briefly.
> [Computer Aided Instruction]

Spolsky, B. (1970). The language teacher in the computer age. In R. C. Lugton (Ed,), Preparing the English teacher as a foreign language teacher: A projection for the 1970's. Center for Curriculum Development, Inc., 401 Walnut St., Philadelphia, PA 19106, 1970. Order no. 2580.

> Not for English, and dated.

S.T.A.R.: General Motors' computerized simple test approach for readability: A tool for improved communications.(No date) Detroit: General Motors. Available from GM Public Relations, 3044 W. Grand Blvd., Detroit, MI 48202.

> An early (pre-1975) text-commentary program which computes the Flesch and Dale-Chall Indices (and grade level) and lists "hi-cal" words (3 or more syllables). The pamphlet lists the BASIC program.
> [Readability]

Stearns, F. (1982). How to select a text editor. Interface Age, 7(1), 108, 111, 112, 114, 116, 18, 164.

> Describes standard and noteworthy features of six programs.
> [Survey of Software]

Stefik, M., Aikins, J., Balzer, R., Benoit, J., Birnbaum, L., Hayes-Roth, F., & Sacerdoti,

E. (1982). The organization of expert systems, a tutorial. Artificial Intelligence, 18(2), 135-73.

> A tutorial. The authors begin with a restricted class of problems that admit a very simple organization. To make this organization feasible the input data must be static, reliable and the solution space must be small enough to search exhaustively. These assumptions are then relaxed, one at a time, in case study of ten more sophisticated prescriptions. The first cases deal with unreliable and time-varying data. Other cases show techniques for creating and reasoning with abstract solution spaces and multiple lines of reasoning. The prescriptions are compared for their coverage and illustrated by expert systems.
> [Design of Software]

Stibic, V. (1980). A few remarks on the user-friendliness of online systems, Journal of Information Science, 2, 277ff.

> Discussion of the need for operator language flexibility for potential users who are not machine oriented.
> [Human Factors]

Stibic, V. (1982). Tools of the mind: Techniques and methods for intellectual work. Amsterdam: North-Holland.

> A general survey of current information technology with a chapter on word processing. Valuable because it puts word processing into a broad context and thereby suggests a wide range of uses for microcomputers beyond text entry and editing. Stibic gives practical, concrete suggestions, so that the book avoids much of the silliness of party-line futurism.
> [Communication Systems, Human Factors, Office of Future, Survey of Hardware, Survey of Software]

Stoan, S. K. (1982). Computer searching: A primer for the uninformed scholar. Academe, 68, 10-15.

Straub, D. W. Jr. (1973). The machine and the rainbow: Computers in the full spectrum of the English curriculum. In Proceedings of a 4th Conference on Computers in the Undergraduate Curricula, 216-221.

Stromfors, O., & Jonesjo, L. (1981). The implementation and experiences of a structure-oriented text editor. Proceedings of ACM SIGPLAN/SIGOA Symposium on Text Manipulation, June 1981, 22-27.

> Oriented more toward text editing as it evolved from data processing needs, which might be useful for students doing research papers. Describes the ED3 editor, a screen-oriented editor which uses the idea of a "tree," a preliminary outline, as

the starting place for inserting blocks of text. The command language seems to be a bit cryptic for students, but the idea might be emulated in a more "user-friendly" environment. (It is written in Pascal, and might be portable.) It can handle simple pictures and formatted data records too. Examples are given.
[Design of Software]

Sturridge, H. (1981). A lesson in computer lessons. Computer Management, March 1981, 28-9.

Current state of the art in computer-based training is discussed.
[Computer Aided Instruction]

Su, S. Y. W., & Moore, R. L. (1972). Discourse synthesis, analysis and their application to CAI. Communication Sciences Laboratory Quarterly Report, 10(1), Gainesville, FL: University of Florida. (ERIC Document Reproduction Service No. ED 087 066)

The bulk of this paper is about teaching computers to read. The computer (an IBM Coursewriter III, at the University of Florida), given a lexicon and a phrase structure or dependency grammar, should be able to process semantic content in varying syntactic forms. The focus is on getting the computer to "comprehend" at the paragraph level. This work is tied to computer-aided journalism instruction, comparable to that of Bishop and Halpern, above (Bishop is in fact cited several times): the facts that make up individual "stories" are stored, as well as predictable syntactic and organizational structures and stylistic judgments (e.g., it looks for repetition, cliches, weak nouns, etc.); a student, given a certain set of facts, writes a news story and the computer analyses it according to the "rules of journalistic discourse" and provides feedback. At the point this paper was produced, the study was still in experimental stages. No provision seems to be made for processing inappropriate grammar; the students are expected to have the fundamentals down.
[Computer Aided Instruction]

Sweeney, G. P. (1979). Microprocessors in communications. Journal of Information Science, 1, 93-105.

Not on writing as such but on telecommunications.
[Communication Systems]

Szanser, A. J. (1970). Automatic error-correction in natural languages. Information Storage and Retrieval, 5(4), 169-174.

Taylor, E. C., & Diamond, R. M. (1966). Use of programmed instruction in a freshman composition course: A feasibility study. Coral Gables, FL: Miami University, University College.

Probably too old to be useful.

Teitelman, W. A. (1977). A display oriented programmer's assistant. Proceedings of the Fifth International Joint Conference on Artificial Intelligence, 905-915.

Not an article on writing environments, but on programming environments; in particular, a programming environment which makes use of windowing, menus, and a mouse (a pointing device) to allow the user to manage simultaneous tasks with greater ease, and to move between these tasks when necessary. A sample session is described and illustrated.
[Design of Software]

Thames, A. M. (1972). CAI and English: A tentative relationship. In Proceedings of the 1972 Conference on Computers in Undergraduate Curricula, 305-310. Atlanta, GA: Southern Regional Education Board.
[Computer Aided Instruction]

Thomas, J. C. (1978). A design-interpretation of natural English with applications to man-computer interaction. International Journal of Man-Machine Studies, 125.

Thompson, N. (1978) Computers: The super multi-media resource. English Journal, 67(91), 98-102.

Jazzy, but not too much substance.

Thorelli, L. E. (1962). Automatic correction of errors in text. BIT, 2, 45-62.
[Spelling Checkers]

Toch, T. (1982). Sophisticated microcomputers used to teach students to write. Education Week, February 2, 1982, 12-16.

A useful introductory newspaper article, bringing to the attention of teachers the "huge potential" in using microcomputers for writing instruction, a "largely undeveloped field," but not a report of any study currently underway, nor an attempt to provide "hard evidence" for the hopes raised. The focus is on elementary and secondary education, but the kinds of potential discussed are equally relevant to college level writing. Several people whose work in this area has been significant are quoted--Colette Daiute of Columbia University Teachers College, Robert Caldwell of the University of Texas Health Science Center in Dallas, Owen Thomas of University of California, Irvine, Shirley Keran of Minnesota Education Computing Consortium, and several others. According to this article, the United Nations International School and the Santa Monica-Malibu School District are currently using micros for writing--the latter for sentence combining--but the projects are not given in-depth treatment.

[Elementary Writing, Secondary Writing, Testimonial]

Tracey, R. (in press). The word processor and the writing process. Forthcoming in *T. H. E. Journal*. Available from the author, English Department, Cerritos Community College, Norwalk, CA 90650.

Introductory assessment of the role of word processors in the writing process which does not, however, present any specific methodology for their use in the classroom. Makes use of a variety of testimonial references from professional writers and publishers on the benefits of word processing for writing; students, it is assumed, will derive the same benefits. Breezy, but with a good awareness of the limitations of current CAI for English.
[Testimonial, Computer Aided Instruction]

Tucker, A. B. J. (1979). *Text processing: Algorithms, languages, and applications*. New York: Academic Press, Inc.

Turba, T. N. (1979). General syntax analyzer (GSA). *ACM SIGPLAN Notices*, 14,(12), 92-109.

Not useful. This is a system for parsing and analyzing *computer* language syntax.

Turba, T. N. (1981). Checking for spelling and typographical errors in computer-based text. *ACM SIGPLAN Notices*, 16(6), 51-60.

A fine review article on dictionary design. It is quite technical. The general user of a word processor which has a spelling-checker need not read this, and it doesn't provide help on deciding which one to buy.
[Spelling Checkers, Dictionary]

Umberger, D. W. (1981). Plan ahead when considering a word processing operation. *The Office*, 93(6), 118, 120, 122.

Umberger outlines things to remember when setting up a word-processing operation, some of which will be relevant for creating writing labs or classrooms which use word processors. In particular, he mentions that the typical writing surface is too high (29" from the floor) for operators, encouraging fatigue and low production; the optimal height is 26" and should be adjustable; this is a typical problem in adapting desks, which an educational institution already has, to be word processing stations.
[Human Factors]

University of Michigan Computing Center Word Processing Project. (1982). *Academic authoring requirements*. Unpublished paper available from the University of Michigan

Computer Center, 1075 Beal Ave., Ann Arbor, MI 48109, 20 pp.

> Survey of what professors and others on campus need in order to write articles, books and similar materials on computers. The survey included issues such as the lack of secretarial support, the need to assume that professors work at home, the office, and the library. The focus is on invention, organization to clarify, and development as pre-writing stages, organization to present ideas to an audience, drafting, and review. The project assumed that the author would range freely among those tasks, and that authors' styles could vary widely.
> [Case Study]

University of Michigan Computing Center Word Processing Project. (1982). Authoring system specifications. Unpublished paper available from the University of Michigan Computer Center, 1075 Beal Ave., Ann Arbor, MI 48109.

> Sections include user interface, esp. windows, menus, the screen manger, document (or file) manager, layout and format, including menus to select choices and a format library, the text editor (50 pp.), the printing control system. These go into more detail than the user of a word processor would need, but they clearly set out the complexity of such a system.
> [Design of Software]

University of Michigan Computing Center Word Processing Project. (1982). Proposal for prototype authoring system. Unpublished paper available from the University of Michigan Computing Center, 1075 Beal Avenue, Ann Arbor, MI 48109.

> The proposed system is described. Its main components are to be (1) an "idea tree grower," (2) a manager of annotations by the author or by others, e.g., peer critics, (3) a summary generator to pick up opening sentences in paragraphs, headings, or other items tagged by the author, and (4) a tool to manage bibliographies. The system is to work on an IBM PC, which can work alone or be linked to Michigan's 370/143 or Amdahl 5860. The model includes "the block" (piece of text), "the set" (ordered list of blocks or other sets), "the tags" (to pick up a hierarchy of blocks), and user-defined windows, in any of which editing is possible.
> [Design of Software, Communication Systems]

Van Campen, J. A. (1970). Effectiveness of various computer-based instructional strategies in language teaching. (Final report No. AD-735 964) Stanford, CA: Stanford University, California Institute for Mathematical Studies in Social Science. (Available from National Technical Information Service, Springfield, VA: 22151)

Van Campen, J. A. (1971). Towards the automatic generation of programmed foreign-language instructional materials. (Report No. TR-163) Stanford CA: Stanford University Institute for Mathematical Studies in Social Science.

Van Dam, A., & Rice, D. E. (1971). On-line editing: A survey. Computer Surveys 3(3), 93-114.

> An interesting and important article. Even though it is "old," the systems they describe are nearly identical to those being sold in 1983. The command features, the handling, and so on have not gotten very far. For our purposes, the ready availability of screen or document editors, rather than only line editors, is important.
> [Survey, Design of Software]

Vasdi, P. (1978). How an author learned to program and found a new freedom. Canadian Datasystems, 10(11), 28, 32.

> Actually, the author didn't learn to program; he learned to use a text processing system to generate 2000 pages of technical documentation. It's mainly anecdotal. Vasdi speculates on desirable additional features, most of which are probably available in some form or another by now.
> [Testimonial]

Vaysey, H. (1980). Playing with words: Word processing. Computer Management, 14-20.

Vendor, industry help produce employable high school graduates with trendy WP skills (1982). Data Management 20(3), 34-5.

> Minority students in an urban high school learn word processing as a trade and for college preparation, via the Gould Ocean Systems Division. They also have access to Gould's word processing facilities on an individual basis. Training manuals and tapes are used.

Von Blum, R., et al. (1982-83). Description of the problem. Unpublished report, Word Processor Writing Project. Available from the Department of Psychology, University of California, Los Angeles, CA 90024.

> Sees the need for "immediate corrective feedback" and an effort to break down writers' problems as being central to effective instruction. Word processors, because they make editing easier, should encourage extensive revision, especially if the computer is programmed to cue revision. It might also help the beginning writer get writing started.
> [Design of Software, Evaluation of Writing]

Von Blum, R., et al. (1982). Practical speculations. Unpublished report, Word Processor Writing Project. Available from the Department of Psychology, University of California, Los Angeles, CA 90024.

Their word processor uses IBM—PC dedicated keys; it defines a word, sentence, and paragraph. The commands are erase, restore, tidy (format). Major programs involve outlines, blocks, search and replace, idea trees, coherence review, etc. The split screen is accessed with a toggle, and the cursor can be on either half. Apparatus for peer review is planned.
[Design of Software, WANDAH]

Von Blum, R., & Cohen, M. (no date). The WANDAH system. Unpublished report, Word Processor Writing Project. Available from the Department of Psychology, University of California, Los Angeles, CA 90024.

The WANDAH system is to help composing, not document production. It has on-line tutorials, extensive menus, and little computer jargon. It allows one or two "windows" (reserved parts of the screen). Pre-writing programs are to foster freewriting, nutshelling, and prompted clustering. Reviewing programs focus on organization, style, and high-frequency grammatical blunders. The system is in UCSD Pascal on an IBM Personal Computer; it is promised for 1983–84.
[WANDAH, Computer Aided Instruction]

Walker, J. H. (1981). The document editor: A support environment for preparing technical documents. Proceedings of the ACM SIGPLAN/SIGOA Symposium on Text Manipulation Association for Computing Machinery], 44–50.

Identifies the requirements for an interactive environment for editing complex documents and describes an initial implementation for the environment.
[Design of Software]

Wall, S., & Taylor, N. (1982). Using interactive computer programs in teaching higher conceptual skills: An approach to instruction in writing. Educational Technology, 22, 13–17.

Calls for computer instruction in writing that would take advantage of the interactive nature of the microcomputer to provide teacher feedback. There are some interesting ideas here, but the the distinction between using the microcomputer as a convenient storage system which allows a student to change her writing in response to a teacher's comments, and using the computer's ability to simulate dialogue between teacher and student somehow gets lost in the course of the article. It is difficult to tell how such teacher feedback on a micro would differ from or be substantially better than traditional handwritten feedback employing the same theoretical principles. The section on "advantages of microcomputers in teaching descriptive writing" presents reasons for doing so, a few of which (that the computer can be viewed as "reader or receiver of the written message," for example) are questionable, both in their accuracy and their desirability. Still, the article proposes a more process-oriented use of microcomputers for writing than do those advocating the usual run of CAI instruction, and is worth looking at on that account alone.

[Computer Aided Instruction]

Walshe, W. A. (1982). The new versatility in text editors. Administrative Management, 43, 38-42.

Describes text editing equipment on the market; discusses features, applications.
[Survey of Software]

Walther, G. H. (1973). The on-line user-computer interface: The effects of interface flexibility, experience, and terminal-type on user satisfaction and performance. Doctoral Dissertation, University of Texas at Austin. (NTIS No. AD-777 314)
[Human Factors]

Walther, G. H., & O'Neill, F. (1974). On-line user-computer interface: The effects of interface flexibility, terminal type, and experience on performance. AFIPS (American Federation of Information Processing Societies) Conference Proceedings, 43, 379-384.

Groups of undergraduate computer science students with varying degrees of experience with interactive computing were taught to use a "flexible" text editing program--i.e., a program in which commands could be abbreviated, optional commands eliminated, and more familiar synonyms for some commands declared if the user preferred. Comparable groups were first introduced to an "inflexible" text editor, identical to the flexible program except that it did not permit the changes described above. All groups were asked to edit (locate and correct errors in) 18 short texts. Individual performance was timed and observed. Conclusions: Students with no previous interactive experience worked faster with the inflexible program; such students appeared to be confused, and subsequently slowed down, by the options of the flexible program. All other students worked faster with the flexible program, but users of the flexible program also make more "syntax errors" in their first trials. (By "syntax errors" the authors refer to errors in program command syntax, not English syntax.) Typing ability did not influence program syntax accuracy; users of CRTs made more program syntax errors than users of teletypewriter terminals.
[Human Factors]

Wang, A. (annual) Index to Computer-Based Learning. Available from Instructional Media Laboratory, University of Wisconsin, Milwaukee.

Updated yearly.
[Survey]

Wang, C. H. C., Mitchel, P. C., Rugh, J. S., & Basheer, B. W. (1977). A statistical method for detecting spelling errors in large data bases. Digest of Papers for Spring COMPCON 77, February-March 1977, 124-128.
[Spelling Checkers]

Ward, S. A., & Terman, C. J. (1980). An approach to personal computing. Digest of Papers, Compcon'80, IEEE, 460-465.

Watkins, N. D. (1977). Computer assisted instruction at Bennett College. In D. A. Christensen (Ed.), Proceedings of 1977 Conference on Computers in the Undergraduate Curricula, 105-108. Iowa City, IA: The University of Iowa. (ERIC Document Reproduction Service No. ED 156 160)

> English grammar is one of the subject areas of computer-assisted instruction at Bennett; math and reading are also being addressed. Common errors such as run-ons and sentence fragments are tackled by means of drill and practice. Some of the procedural details of integrating CAI into college curricula and moving from business-produced to instructor-authored software might be interesting to some, but on the whole the article is not especially relevant.
> [Computer Aided Instruction, Grammar Drill]

Watt, D. (1982) Which computer should a school buy? Popular Computing, 140-144.

> Addressed to those choosing computers for grade school, junior high, or high school. It focuses on several fallacies that often affect such decisions. Furthermore, it points out how the differing purposes which one should have for computers change both with the grade level and from year to year in the same grade level. These changing purposes require, the author argues, quite different choices.
> [Elementary Writing, Secondary Writing, Survey of Software]

Welsch, L. A. (1982). Using electronic mail as a teaching tool. Communications of the ACM, 25, 105-108.

> Electronic mail allowed responses from teacher to student to teacher, and between students. Class was an engineering writing class, with emphasis on process.
> [Communication Systems]

Werner, L. (1981). Word processing. Popular Electronics, 19, August, 29-36.

> Introductory article. Explains differences between electronic typewriters, dedicated word processors, and small business/personal computers with word processing programs, and discusses advantages and disadvantages of each, primarily for business purposes. Desirable hardware features are discussed, along with suggestions for choosing software. A list of major vendors is provided.
> [Design of Hardware]

Where to get well trained word-processing operators? The Office, 95(2), 89, 126.

> Outlines Olsten Temporary Service's model of training people for word processors:

screening and selection of qualified students; offering easy, simple, understandable learning and training methods; and supporting students with a follow-up service. Prospective students must be interested in learning the system, be able to type a minimum of 40 words a minute, and have good understanding of spelling, grammar, punctuation, and other writing basics. The training method involves instruction on the equipment through the use of exercises that simulate assignments the students will work on in their jobs. The process takes four hours a day for four days, a total of 16 hours for the students. If the instructors and staff feel more time is needed, then the training period is extended. The method emphasizes a strong and trusting relationship between the instructor and the student; this helps students gain confidence in using the equipment and eliminates the mystique by simplifying explanations and instructions. After the training, Olsten gives its graduates a hot-line number they can call for help and to reduce confusion in their jobs as they gain experience.
[Office of Future]

Wickmann, D. (1980). An automatic analysis of semantic relationships between words in texts: Factor or cluster analysis--what fits best. ALLC Bulletin, 8(2), 152-165.
[Semantics]

Wilkinson, A. C. (Ed.). (1982). Classroom computers and cognitive science. New York: Academic Press.

Williams, R. L. (1980). Sentence construction with a computer. Creative Computing, 6(4), 52, 54, 56, 58.

What's described here is a BASIC program called ABECEDARIAN, which conjugates a few finite verbs in various tenses, and produces questions and answers using those verbs. Mainly a toy right now, with no apparent educational value, but if anyone is interested, the program is listed. The grammar incorporated into the program is derived from Martin Joos' The English verb: Form and meaning, which "postulates a binary schema which assigns either/or "values" to several features of finite verb predications. In turn, these values can be expressed in decimal numbers . . . all finite predications (verbs) may be described or coded with a five place binary number."
[Syntax]

Wilson, H. A., & Fitzgibbon, N. H. (1970). Practice and perfection: A preliminary analysis of achievement data from the CAI elementary English program. Elementary English, 47(4), 576-580.
[Computer Aided Instruction, Case Study, Elementary Writing]

Wilson, K. (1981). English teachers: Key to computer literacy. English Journal, 70, 50-53.

Well meaning, but vague and uninformed. Examines the "hesitancy, even resistance among educators to create curriculum and teaching techniques expressly designed for a computerized society" and "the function of the English teacher in this surge for a new 'literacy.'" Unfortunately, the article relies on a fundamental misappropriation of the term "computer literacy" which usually means competence over several computer systems (as opposed to "computer adeptness," which means proficiency with the computer one has, but little or no experience generalizing that knowledge and applying it to other systems): "computer literacy renamed is 'computer communication,' and English is the discipline of communication." The pleas for English teachers to instruct students in "the ability to communicate in clear, concise terms in a logical sequence" which is evidently supposed to make us all better programmers; the major differences between the English language and most programming languages is blurred over. Wilson also calls for more exercises in problem-solving skills in English workbooks--not a bad idea, per se, but curious that there's no mention of putting such exercises on a computer. Elementary school oriented; no mention of computer-assisted writing.
[Computer Literacy]

Wimmer, K. E. (1978). Research on human interface considerations for interactive text generation. Conference on Evolutions in Computer Communications, Kyoto, Japan. Amsterdam, Netherlands: North-Holland, 727-32.

Describes how a word processor meshes with operators' cognitive skills and motivations. Forty operators, mostly secretaries, operated word processors both with and without display; their actions were studied for several weeks, 8 hours per day, under normal working conditions. Protocol data were run through evaluation programs to derive and compare operation characteristics for different word processor's, operators, and tasks. Operators answered a set of questionnaires on their working conditions and commented on the word processors' operational aspects. Results are summarized.
[Human Factors]

Wineland, J. A. (1982). Word processing at Carnegie-Mellon University. Cause/Effect, 5, 22-6.

Winkel, B. J. (1983). Word processing for academia. Collegiate Microcomputer, 1, 124-128.

Simple, anecdotal introduction to word processing and its uses in undergraduate settings, all aimed at instructor uses, not student uses.

Winter, F. (1980). College computers in action. CIPS Review, 4, 10-12.

Describes personal computer use at Sheridan College, Ontario, especially the development of a new microcomputer management course, the use of the PET,

computer aided instruction, and word processing.
[Computer Aided Instruction]

Wise. D. (1982).   The fight for desktop space: Micros battle word processors.
InfoWorld, 4(1), 19.

> Discusses the rise of the micro and its effect on office automation.   Now
> software developers have to produce good word processing packages for micros,
> since more offices are demanding computers and word processing power.
> Dedicated systems still work best where word processing plays a predominant role,
> in the office environment, because they are better designed for office work, easier
> to use, and better supported by the companies selling them.
> [Human Factors]

Wisher, R. A. (June 1979).   Improving language skills by computer.   In Annual meeting
of ADCIS.   Dallas, TX: Association for the Development of Computer–Based
Instructional Systems.   (ERIC Document Reproduction Service No. ED 165 710)

> Highlights programs under development at the Navy Personnel Research and
> Development Center in San Diego.   The paper centers around reading skills but
> writing skills are also considered.   Views the computer as "an evaluator and
> instructor of language skills" which "has yet to find its place," though "we know
> that it belongs."   One of the ways it seems to belong is fairly typical: as a
> motivational tool, it offers students "patient," individualized instruction.
>
> The bulk of the paper describes a project under development by Wisher for
> remedial readers (below the sixth grade level).   It uses a DEC PDP-11/45, which
> drives a multi–media learning system.   Skill areas addressed are phonics,
> vocabulary development, and reading comprehension: video cassettes provide a
> "reading theater" in which actors act out a story accompanied by dialogue, and
> any underlined word in the story can be pronounced at the student's request by a
> voice synthesizer.   Reading rate and comprehension are monitored by the
> computer.
>
> The last two pages are devoted to writing instruction on the computer, especially
> to sentence combining routines and paragraph development (by reorganizing a
> given set of sentences into a coherent structure), and to hardware and software
> requirements for computer aided writing instruction; the assumption is you'll want
> an on-line system.   Word processors are not addressed.
> [Sentence Combining Exercises]

Wittig, S. (1974) Three behavioral approaches to the teaching of college–level
composition: Diagnostic tests, contracts and computer–assisted instruction.   In Second
Annual Conference on Research and Technology in College and University Teaching.
(ERIC Document Reproduction Service No. ED 099 887)

An attempt to individualize freshman composition in an experimental course at the University of Texas. After the student is given a diagnostic test of her/his grammar, sentence-combining, and essay capabilities, the instructor outlines sentence, paragraph, and essay objectives for that student. When the student completes these objectives and demonstrates competence in each area, the course ends. Seven instructional computer modules, which may be used independently with a handbook or as supplements to other forms of instruction.
[Sentence Combining Exercises]

Wittig, S. (1978). The computer and the concept of text. Computers and the Humanities, 11. 211-215.

Argues that computer-aided (literary) criticism has emulated only the limited conceptual framework of New Criticism. Advocates instead "a new study of how, and why, and under what conditions, the text is fulfilled with meaning by it readers." Given Wittig's focus in literature, the value (or risks) of subjecting student writing only to New Critical or formalist analysis must be addressed.
[Literary Analysis]

Wittig, S. (1978). DIALOGUE: Project C-BE English drill and practice. Pipeline, 4, 20-22.

Wittig, S. W., & Bracewell, M. (1975). Evaluating computer-assisted instruction in English. In Proceedings of the 1976 Conference on Computers in the Undergraduate Curricula. Ft. Worth, TX: Texas Christian University.
[Computer Aided Instruction]

Wittig, S., Jernigan, J., & Culp, G. H. (1976). The transportation of computer-based instruction in English: Some problems, politics, and possibilities. In T. C. Willoughby (Ed.), Proceedings of the 1976 Conference on Computers in the Undergraduate Curricula. Binghamton, NY: State University of New York at Binghamton.
[Design of Software]

Wolton, D. (1979) Do you love your VDT? Columbia Journalism Review, 18(2), 36-39.

Discusses the reconciliation of VDT (Video Display Terminal) technology with press philosophy and the need to process information.
[Journalism]

Wong, R. L., Reno, J. D., Hain, T. C., Platt, R. C., Gaynon, P. S., & Joseph, D. M. (1980). Profile of a dictionary compiled from scanning over one million words of surgical pathology narrative text. Computers and Biomedical Research, 13(4), 382-402.

Woodruff, E. (1982) "Computers and the composing process: An examination of computer-writer interaction." In J. Lawlor (Ed.), Computers in composition instruction. Los Alamitos, CA: SWRL Education Research and Development.

> Written with Carl Bereiter and Marlene Scardamalia and is similar to the material found in the Woodruff, Bereiter and Scardamalia Journal of Educational Technology Systems article, below. Primarily, it describes CAC (Computer-Assisted Composition) -1 and -2, the different purposes of each, the different methods of interaction between computer and student, and the varying results. CAC-1 provides basic assistance for an argument plan, producing the next sentence, changing words, and checking words one is unsure about. CAC-2, while supposedly designed to direct students' attention to "higher level concerns" than CAC-1, is more interruptive of the writing process (it automatically intervenes with a question about content, reasoning, evidence or reader reaction at the end of each sentence). EXPLORE, a program which includes a data base for a paper (on whether TV is a good influence on young people) containing 154 "pro" and 154 "con" statements, in varying styles and voices ("OK," weak, exaggerated, unbelievable, unclear, wordy, or jazzy), is then discussed. Students can thus construct "bad" as well as "good" compositions and learn why wordy or jazzy writing is problematic. Something like this might also be a way to learn about different rhetorical requirements for different audiences, although here "OK" is really the only "OK" style to select. EXPLORE, like the CAC programs, is designed to "minimize cognitive burdens."
> [CAC, Computer Aided Instruction, Invention, Elementary Writing, Secondary Writing]

Woodruff, E., Bereiter, C., & Scardamalia, M. (1981-82). On the road to computer assisted compositions. Journal of Educational Technology Systems, 10(2), 133-148.

> Two studies aimed primarily at elementary and junior high school students, but with some implications for college composition. The first study used a program called CAC-1 (for Computer-Aided Composition), a simplified word processing program written in BASIC and implemented in the fall of 1979 on a 32K Commodore PET personal computer. In addition to word processing features, the program has writing help menus designed for "procedural facilitation" to reduce the cognitive demands of writing yet still allow the writer to retain control of content. CAC-1's writing help came when the student pressed the help key or when the keyboard was inactive for more than twenty seconds. The menu provided organizational cues for following an "argument plan", gave prompts to encourage additional writing, and helped the student play back the text, change words and quit when s/he wanted. Students who were offered help when they didn't want it (i.e, after twenty seconds) could answer "no" and thereby increase the time the keyboard could remain inactive, without eliciting an offer of help, by five seconds.

The findings of the first study indicate that "children were able and willing to work interactively with the computer during the composing process," (p. 139). However, students often used organizational cues as a list of things to include, a "recipe" for their paper: "while the subjects appear to find the program helpful for organization and cueing of content, it did not seem to have actually engaged the students in a higher-level consideration of composition choices," (p. 141). A second study, therefore, was undertaken.

In the second study, a modified version of CAC-1 was used, CAC-2, which relied on a more active intervention in the composing process and a different type of help, what the authors call "response-sensitive" questions. These questions were actually prompts for thinking about a topic, and thus the scorers' assessment of CAC-2 compositions as being less well thought out is predictable; in fact, students were being asked to respond to prewriting questions in the middle of composing, something that would affect anyone's organizing, especially considering that the interaction in CAC-2 was compulsory and occurred at the end of each sentence the student typed (though the student could dismiss the question or put it "on hold" if s/he wished). Desirability of such interference at the college level, during composing, is dubious, but there is still much of interest in these studies for individuals seeking to enhance the word processor as a heuristic tool.
[CAC, Computer Aided Instruction, Case Study, Elementary Writing]

Woods, W. A. (1970). Transition network grammars for natural language analysis. Communications of the ACM, 13, 591–606.

A "classic" piece on the transition network grammar, now widely used in many applications for question-answering, artificial intelligence, and natural language processing.
[Syntax]

Woods, W. A. (1977). Lunar rocks in natural English: Explorations in natural language question answering. In A. Zampulli (Ed.), Linguistic Structures Processing. Amsterdam: North-Holland, 521–70.

Full, technical, but introductory account of the "Augmented transition network" (ATN) grammar, a further development along the lines of Woods' earlier paper.
[Syntax]

Word processing equipment (1978). Graphic Communications World, 11(12), 10.

Table of 100 systems.
[Survey of Hardware]

Word processing: How will it shape the student as a writer? (1982). Forum in Classroom Computer News, 3., 24ff.

Differing views on the use and impact of word processing in K–12 classrooms.
[Testimonial]

<u>Word processing: Selected display keyboards</u> (1980). Datapro Research 1980.

Evaluation of Lanier Text Editors LTE-1 and -2, the Vydec 1146, 1200, and 1400 Word Processing Systems, the IBM Office System 6 Information Processors, and the Xerox Page 850 Display. Selected from Datapro Reports on Office Systems.
[Human Factors]

<u>Word processing systems user ratings</u> (1980). Datapro Research.

Detailed analysis of ratings given by over 1000 word processing users on 75 makes and models of equipment. Over 120 statistical and narrative entries for each system, summary tables. These are selected from Datapro's Reports on Word Processing.
[Survey]

Word processing training: Alternative approaches (1981). <u>Automated Office Systems</u>, <u>1</u>(2), 1–4.

Outlines the various approaches in word-processing training––Vendor training packages, augmenting of vendor training packages, developing of one's own training program, and having a training firm develop your training program––offering the disadvantages and advantages of each and suggesting how to implement and augment each choice. It also charts, for those interested in developing their own training program, the advantages and disadvantages of various training methods: lecture, self-study, one-on-one, programmed, and interactive (a combination of programmed and one-on-one).
[Office of Future]

Word/text processing––A look at recently introduced systems. <u>Canadian Datasystems</u>, <u>12</u>(4), 37–62.

Words (International Word Processing Association Spring Symposium) (1980). <u>New Yorker</u>, March 10, <u>56</u>, 37–38.

A free-wheeling discussion among educational computing "experts," participants in a special session of the 1982 National Educational Computing Conference, of issues surrounding computers in education: computer literacy, equity issues, teacher re-training, software development, software piracy, etc.

Wrege, R., & Watt, D. (1982). Forum on educational computing. <u>Popular Computing</u>, November, 132–141.

Wresch, W. (1982). Prewriting, writing, and editing by computer. Paper presented at the annual meeting of the Conference on College Composition and Communication, San Francisco. (ERIC Document Reproduction Service No. ED 213 045)

Wresch, W. (1982). Computers in English class: Finally beyond grammar and spelling drills. College English, 44, 483–490.

> Reports on Burns, above, for invention, Wresch's own program, for paper organization, older programs for sentence embedding and specificity of word choice, and Cohen's HOMER, above, for surface editing.
> [Survey, Invention, HOMER]

Wresch. W. (Ed.) (1983). A Writer's tool: The computer in composition instruction. Manuscript submitted for publication.

> Contains three major sections with articles written by knowledgeable writing teachers and administrators who have developed computer–assisted writing instruction packages: 1) Prewriting Approaches (contributions from H. Burns, Rodrigues, Schwartz, and Wresch; 2) Editing and Grammar Programs (Kiefer and Smith, Cohen, Lanham, Southwell), and Word Processing and Unified Systems (Bridwell and Ross, Marcus, Daiute, Von Blum and Cohen, Selfe, and Neuwirth). Includes an annotated bibliography developed by Bruce Appleby. An excellent introduction to the possibilities for computers in writing classes, secondary through college.
> [Survey, Composing Processes]

Wresch, W. (1983). Computers and composition instruction: An update. College English, manuscript submitted for publication, 11 pp.

> Updates Wresch's earlier article (1982) by reviewing rapid developments in the field in one year's time.
> [Survey of Software]

Wresch, W. (1983). Computer essay generation. The Computing Teacher, March, 10, 63–65.

> Describes a pre–writing program to generate a rough 4–paragraph essay with different rhetorical approaches.
> [Invention]

Yerkey, A. N. (1976). The retrieval of rhetorical topoi: A computer–assisted system for the invention of lines of argument and associated data (Doctoral dissertation, Kent State University). Dissertation Abstracts International, 37, 2501–A.

> Develops and tests an audience analysis program based on Aristotle's eide topoi

and his criteria for happiness. The topoi work well, but the criteria need more thought; the survey Yerkey uses to show that the criteria are still valid suffers from a lack of realistic choices. Students get to choose between "wealth," "Stalin," "sin," and "boulder," for example; it's rather obvious what they'd choose. Humanistic criteria for happiness (e.g., "intellectual/spiritual/personal growth," "religion," "learning") are not offered.

Program runs on an extensive data base and needs (1) a list of the most salient topics which concern Americans about the chosen issue; (2) a list of information sources; (3) a list of the consequences of adopting or not adopting proposals connected with the issues; (4) a list under each consequence of materials with which to construct lines of argument (i.e., why the consequences are good, bad, etc.). Yerkey has programmed such a base for one minor liberal-arts-type moral issue, and notes it would take an incredible amount of time and memory to build such a base for all issues. The idea is certainly interesting, but the execution of the idea seems lacking. The applicability of the happiness criteria, the all-inclusive data base, and the experimental design.
[Case Study]

Zacchei, D. (1982). The adventures and exploits of the dynamic STORY MAKER and TEXTMAN: Or, how Johnny learns to understand what he reads. Classroom Computer News, 2, 28-30, 76, 77.

Summarizes the genesis and basic operation of STORY MAKER and TEXTMAN, described in more detail in Rubin, above. Important to note is that Zaccher sees the advantage this has as a computer activity (it was originally a cardboard cut-out activity done on a bulletin or cork board) is that students can get a printout. The resulting enthusiasm is comparable, for elementary students, to having their work "published." Otherwise no clear rationale is presented here for why this is a computer writing activity (though a clear rationale could be formulated). The "software considerations" section does not really focus on issues related to the implementation of this educational tool as computer software so much as it describes the educational goals of STORY MAKER and TEXTMAN.
[STORY MAKER, TEXTMAN]

Zamora, A. (1978). Control of spelling errors in large data bases. The Information Age in Perspective. Proceedings of the ASIS Annual Meeting, White Plains, NY: Knowledge Industry Publications, Inc., 364-7.

Technical article on what spelling error detection techniques work best in large data bases. Chemical Abstracts Service's data base served as a test case. Conclusion: a technique which uses dictionary lookup and prefix and suffix extension of that dictionary seems the best so far.
[Spelling Checkers]

Zinsser, W. (1983). Writing with a word processor. New York: Harper Colophon.

Informal testimonial. Predicts that word processors will draw people into writing, partly because of the phenomenon of seeing their own text on the screen (rather than going through a step where someone else does the typing). Many of the technical details he mentions, however, relate rather specifically to the IBM Displaywriter. He gives some helpful hints on saving files, protecting disks, etc. Zinsser likes to have one paragraph perfect before going to the next; his main strategy for editing others' writing is to bracket questionable words or passages—in both cases, word processors are ideal. He does give hints about other writing methods.

[Testimonial]

Zoller, P. T. (1975). Composition and the computer. Unpublished report of computer programs in remedial English. (ERIC Document Reproduction Service No. ED 127 611)

Remedial CAI. Grammar and syntax programs were used with fifteen students at the University of California, Riverside, who did at least one program a week on the computer, and met once a week for a two hour writing workshop. It wasn't possible to assess the experiment's effect upon writing (or, moreover, to distinguish between the effect of the CAI and that of the writing workshop), but student response was positive. The students wanted punctuation programs, too. A logical extension of this might be developed by PLATO, others.

[Computer Aided Instruction]

Relevant Journals

AEDS (Association for Educational Data Systems) Bulletin. Association for Educational Data Systems, 1201 Sixteenth Street, N.W., Washington, DC 20036.

AEDS Monitor. Association for Educational Data Systems, 1201 Sixteenth Street, N. W., Washington, DC 20036.

ALLC (Association of Literary and Linguistic Computing) Bulletin. Subscription address: Dr. J. L. Dawson, Literary and Linguistic Computing Centre, Sidgwick Site, Cambridge CB3 9 DA England.

American Journal of Computational Linguistics. Association for Computational Linguistics, Secretary-Treasurer, D. E. Walker, SRI International, 333 Ravenswood Avenue, Menlo Park, CA 94025. Editorial address: G. E. Heidorn, IBM Thomas J. Watson Research Center, P. O. Box 218, Yorktown Heights, NY 10598.

Apple Education News. Apple Computer, 10260 Bandley Drive, Cupertino, CA 95014.

Bell Systems Technical Journal. American Telephone and Telegraph Co., 600 Mountain Avenue, Murray Hill, NJ 07974.

> Most of the articles here are very technical, intended to disseminate information on hardware and software developments to the technicians themselves. Unless you're really deeply involved with design of your equipment, they'll be little of interest here. Much of the Bell Labs material of general importance is published elsewhere, where it can be directed to a wider audience.

BYTE. P. O. Box 590, Martinsville, NJ 08836

> Calls itself "the small systems journal;" publishes articles relating to all aspects of microcomputer systems, from technical details to programming hints. Educational uses of microcomputers are occasionally addressed. You need to be beyond the "beginner" stage in understanding computers to make use of what BYTE offers, but if you're willing to study the first few issues carefully, you can move yourself beyond that stage. BYTE probably provides the most thorough reviews of new equipment available, so it's good to consult if you're considering acquiring one or more microcomputers and don't want to have to be totally dependent on the advice of your computer center.

Classroom Computer News. 341 Mt. Auburn Street, Watertown, MA 02172.

RELEVANT JOURNALS

Collegiate Microcomputer.

Communications of the ACM (Association for Computing Machinery). Association for Computing Machinery, 11 West 42nd St., New York, NY 10036.

Provides useful, fairly detailed technical information on text editor design, spelling checkers, natural language syntax, etc. Most of the articles are 5-7 pages long, but some can be longer. A forum for experimental research, carefully designed, and is thus good to balance against information derived from anecdotal reports and practi cal but uncontrolled experience in the classroom. Occasionally the focus is educational, but the journal is not specifically designed to address educational needs.

Compute. P. O. Box 5406, Greensboro, NC 27403.

Computer Using Educators (CUE) Newsletter. C.U.E. Membership, P. O. Box 18547, San Jose, CA 95158.

Computers and Education. Pergamon Press, Ltd. Heddington Hill Hall, Oxford OX3 OBW England.

Computers and the Humanities. North-Holland Publishing Co., P. O. Box 211, 1000 AE. Amsterdam, Netherlands.

College level publication for those interested in programs and re search on computer applications across the humanities.

Computers, Reading and Language Arts (CRLA). Gerald H. Block, Ed., P. O. Box 13039, Oakland, CA 94661.

New. Looking for manuscripts, readers. Emphasis is on classroom teaching implications; more for elementary and secondary schools than for postsecondary education.

The Computing Teacher, ICCE, Dept. 58, 135 Education, University of Oregon, Eugene, OR 97408. 9 issues/yr. $16.50.

Largely for K-12. Has a regular section on CAI programs in the humanities and one entitled "Computers in the Teaching of English."

RELEVANT JOURNALS

CourseWare.

Creative Computing. P. O. Box 789-M, Morristown, NJ 07960.

Datapro Reports on Word Processing. Datapro Research. Available from 1977--$425.00 per year in 1982.

> Looseleaf monthly report on hardware, software, services (including dictation equipment), vendors, and standards. Datapro also publishes several separate studies each year on topics such as keyboards.

Educational Computer. P. O. Box 535, Cupertino, CA 95015.

Educational Technology. 140 Sylvan Avenue, Englewood Cliffs. NJ 07632.

> Geared primarily to elementary and secondary school concerns, and helpful for teachers and administrators trying to plan principled use of technology as opposed to haphazard acquisition; it also often has useful articles of general interest. Material is readable and short (3-7 pages), and is usually more concerned with showing teachers how to apply technology to their needs than with explaining how that technology works. Frequently concerned with microcomputers these days, and how their accessibility is changing the face of CAI.

Electronic Education. P.O. Box 20221, Tallahassee, FL 32304.

Electronic Learning. Scholastic, Inc., 902 Sylvan Avenue, Englewood Cliffs. NJ 07632.

The Finite String Newsletter

> Part of American Journal of Computational Linguistics: see above.

Focus: Teaching English Language Arts. Department of English Language and Literature, Ellis Hall 385, Ohio University, Athens, OH 45701.

> Upcoming issue will have articles on "practical and theoretical possibilities for the use of computers in the teaching of English."

Hands On! Technical Education Research Centers, 8 Eliot Street, Cambridge, MA 02138.

RELEVANT JOURNALS

IEEE Transactions on Professional Communication. Institute of Electrical and Electronics Engineers, 345 E. 47th St., New York, NY 10017.

> Much of the Bell Labs work, especially on WRITER'S WORKBENCH, is published here. Addresses common issues of text production in the electronic age-- readability formulas, spelling checkers, the ergonomics of text editors, etc.--for people who have access to text processing equipment in their professions, rather than for students acquiring writing experience. Describes hardware and software features and functioning more often than it reports specific research results.

Index to Computer-Based Learning. A. Wang, Ed. Available from Instructional Media Laboratory, University of Wisconsin, Milwaukee 53201.

Infoworld: The Newsweekly for Microcomputer Users. 375 Cochituate Road, Box 880. Framingham, MA 01701.

> A weekly newspaper devoted to short articles on microcomputer hardware and software, with an In Focus section devoted to longer discussions. The magazine devotes relatively little space specifically to microcomputing in education, but is one of the best sources for keeping up on technical and business developments in microcomputing. New word processing packages are routinely described and reviewed. Most articles are not too technical. There is also plenty of outright gossip.

Interface Age. 16704 Marquardt Avenue, Cerritos, CA 90701.

The Journal of Computer Based Instruction. Association for the Development of Computer-Based Instructional Systems, Computer Center, Western Washington University, Bellingham, WA 98225.

The Journal of Courseware Review. The Apple Foundation P. O. Box 28426, San Jose, CA 95159.

> Apple courseware.

Journal of Educational Technology Systems. Baywood Publishing Co., Inc., 120 Maine Street, Farmingdale, NY 11735.

Microcomputers in Education. 5 Chapel Hill Drive, Fairfield, CT 06432.

Microcomputing. P. O. Box 997, Farmingdale, NY 11737.

Micro-scope. JEM Research, Discovery Park, University of Victoria, Box 1700, Victoria, B. C. V8W 2Y2 Canada.

Microsift Reviews. Northwest Regional Educational Laboratory, 300 S.W. Sixth Avenue, Portland, OR 97204.

Personal Computing. P. O. Box 2941, Boulder, CO 80321.

Pipeline. CONDUIT, P. O. Box 388, University of Iowa, Iowa City, 52244. Published quarterly.

> CONDUIT collects, evaluates and distributes high quality computer-based instructional materials for higher education. Pipeline accepts unsolicited articles, but usually treats a special topic with each issue. CONDUIT has distributed over 200 microcomputer packages a month--they will do some reworking of programs and documentation; they have a guide for authors.

Popular Computing. P. O. Box 307, Martinsville, NJ 08836.

> Basically the TIME magazine version of BYTE (monthly, but with a similar format). Provides "news" about computers rather than detailed technical information. It used to be aimed at computer hobbyists, but is now turning more toward business applications. Some business concerns (e.g., negotiating computer contracts, insurance information) overlap with educational needs, and educational software is occasionally reviewed.

School Microware Reviews. Dresden Associates, Box 246, Dresden, ME 04342.

Softside. Box 68. Milford, NH 03055.

Software Review. Microform Review, 520 Riverside Avenue, Westport, CT 06880

T. H. E. (Technological Horizons in Education) Journal. Information Synergy, Inc., P.O. Box 992, Acton, MA 01720.

> Oriented more toward college level educational concerns than Educational Technology but a larger proportion of the articles seem to be anecdotal or

speculative. Articles intended to provide guidelines for others are occasionally helpful. Some writing and word processing material is being published here; it's not exclusively CAI.

User's: The MECC Instructional Computer Newsletter. 2520 North Broadway Drive, St. Paul, MN 55113.

The Writing Instructor Freshman Writing Program, University of Southern California, Los Angeles, CA 90007.

Summer 1983 issue has articles on computers.

Glossary

q.v. = see entry or entries in the bibliography under the author's name

algorithm	systematic procedure, e.g., a computer program
authoring system	programs which allow instructors (or others) to create sequences of lessons or exercises
artificial intelligence	(AI) computer science field which tries to program computers to simulate human intelligence; much AI work involves analysis of natural language
back up	copy of a file, sometimes on a physically different disk, in case one fails
BASIC	an elementary programming language, available on most microcomputers
batch processing	when a program (or set of them) is run all at once, without intervention by the users, as opposed to interactive processing
bit	contraction of "binary digit"; a single piece of electronic information
block	electronically marked part of a text; less commonly, a technical term referring to the physical way information is put on a floppy disk
block movement	command in a word processing program to copy a block to where the cursor is and erase the block from its old place
byte	eight bits which together can represent one character (letter or number)
CAC	Computer-Assisted Composition, program described by E. Woodruff (q.v.)
CAI	computer-aided instruction
Cathode ray tube	viewscreen similar to a TV set; see CRT
CBT	computer-based training
central processing unit	see CPU

chip	very small electronic circuit built on silicon; a whole computer's CPU can be on one chip
command	an instruction, generally in a special language or from a short list of English words, which tells the computer what to do (e.g., "erase")
command line	list at top or bottom of screen of what commands are possible; sometimes a list of options or "parameters" which comes after a command word
compiler	a computer program that translates a program written in a special language (e.g., BASIC) into simpler instructions which the computer proper can operate on
computer literacy	the idea that students need to understand and to have had experience using computers as part of their education
COMPUPOEM	program written by S. Marcus (q.v.)
CONDUIT	an organization which distributes computer programs and CAI materials
continuous forms	see form
courseware	software used for instruction
CP/M	an operating system available for many microcomputers, written by Digital Research, the de facto standard for small 8-bit business microcomputers
CPU	central processing unit--a small chip of silicon, where the commands are executed, the most important part of the computer
CREATE	programs written by H. Burns (q.v.)
CRT	cathode ray tube--the viewscreen, similar to a TV set, that most microcomputers have to display text, pictures, etc.
cursor	the one-character block (or other symbol) which shows where the next typed character will appear on the screen
daisy wheel	printing device with characters on little sticks attached to a central spindle, in a daisy pattern

GLOSSARY

database	a usually huge, electronically stored file of information, both entered and recovered in a structured format, which can be searched and recalled selectively, and which often covers a limited area (e.g. student's records)
data processing	general term for what computers do; connotes the handling of numbers rather than texts
dedicated key	see "function key"
dedicated word processor	a hardware and software combination which does word processing, but which cannot run other kinds of programs
delete	word processing command meaning erase
DICTION	one program in WRITER'S WORKBENCH
disk	flat piece of material in some kind of holder which can electronically store texts, programs or other data and which can be plugged into a computer
disk drive	hardware device which holds hard or floppy disks and turns them around under a "read-write head" so that information on the disk can be found by the computer; works similarly to a cassette tape player
diskette	small (usually 5 1/4" or 8") disk for a microcomputer
display-oriented	a program which shows information a whole screenful at a time, instead of one line at a time; also called "screen-oriented," as opposed to "line-oriented"
document markup	instructions a writer or editor writes by hand on a typed text; generally for someone else to use to change the text with a word processor
DOS	a disk operating system, available for various microcomputers (e.g., "PC-DOS" for the IBM, "Apple-DOS," etc.)
dot matrix	printing system where characters are formed by patterns of dots
drill and practice	programmed learning (whether computer-based or not) aiming to teach a well-defined skill such as punctuation.
electronic bulletin board	a program and associated files which let users of various

computers leave messages on one central computer for anyone to see

electronic mail — an electronic bulletin board that also lets you send mail privately to anyone whose electronic address you know.

EDP — electronic data processing--general term for what computers do to information, including texts

EPISTLE — programs written by L. Miller, and others (q.v.)

ergonomics — the scientific study of how to make the work place more comfortable and amenable to efficient work, including topics such as keyboard layout, lighting, and whether chairs are comfortable; see human factors

ETUDE — an interactive editor and formatter developed at MIT

EYEBALL — a program written by D. Ross (q.v.)

file — an organized series of characters (or other information) which a computer can find, display, etc.

firmware — programs (or other information) physically attached to a computer; essentially the same as software

Flesch Index — a simple formula which translates information about word and sentence lengths into a grade-level, denoting "readability"

floppy disk — small (usually 5 1/4" or 8") disk made out of plastic and held in a square paper envelope; used in a microcomputer

form — physically connected paper that feeds through the printer; it is torn off at the perforations into separate sheets after printing

format — word processing command to set margins, justify the text right and left, and other layout functions

frame — text, stored in a computer, which fills the TV screen

function key — on the keyboard, a key separate from the numbers and letters, which lets a complicated command be given at one time (e.g., "erase")

global search and replace — word processing command that will look for one specified string of letters or words, and put a second string in its place every time the former is found.

graphics capability   hardware which can use programs to draw pictures or lines on the TV screen

Gunning Fog Index   a simple formula which translates information about word and sentence lengths into a grade-level, denoting "readability"

hard copy   jargon, means printed text

hard disk   small disk and driving system for microcomputer; always having at least 10 times as much storage space as a floppy disk, which works about 10 times as fast as a floppy disk, and which is attached permanently to the computer

hardware   the physical apparatus of a computer; the hardware for microcomputers is a keyboard, display screen, disk drive or cassette and the central processing unit (CPU)

HOMER   program written by M. Cohen (q.v.)

human factors design   efforts to study how people work most comfortably with computers (and other machines); ergonomics

information processing   general term for what computers do, especially when the data are texts or words, rather than numbers; also involves the transmitting of information from one computer to another

input   information (programs, data, texts) which is electronically sent to the central processing unit, e.g., by typing

insert   word processing command that puts typed characters into the text, generally by electronically moving other characters out of the way

interactive processing   a program which is run from a terminal while the user is waiting, which the user can interrupt; often such programs pause and ask for more complicated instructions from the user

interface   the electronic link between parts of a computer, e.g., between the keyboard and the central processing unit; metaphorically, the link between the computer and the human who uses it.

GLOSSARY

i/o

input and output--most commonly between the CPU and other parts of the computer

joystick

a device which moves the cursor around the TV screen; a vertical stick in a box is moved to indicate the direction of the cursor; usually used in games

jump

word processing command to move the cursor to a specific place in the text, e.g., 3 paragraphs down

K

about 1,000 bytes of memory capacity

keystroke

the pressing of a keyboard key; a basic measure of the time and effort needed to get a text into a computer

line editor

a word processing program that works on only one line at a time, as opposed to display-oriented or screen-oriented word processing programs

machine language

a series of on/off signals that a computer understands

macro

a fixed series of commands which the user can type in once and then use again by hitting a special function key, or giving only one command, e.g., a routinely-used printing format for bibliographies

mainframe

a very large and expensive computer such as operated by university computer centers

mass storage

general term for a device (usually a disk or tape) that remembers electronic data even if the power is shut off.

menu

list of choices presented on the TV screen with instructions on how to pick the desired one

microcomputer

physically small computer, from desk-top size down; uses a microprocessor as its central processing unit

microprocessor

central processing unit of a microcomputer (or part of a larger machine); a complex electronic device built on a small piece of silicon which actually executes the commands, instead of merely passing them on to another part of the machine

minicomputer

medium sized computer, about the size of a filing cabinet, but too expensive for a single user to own; almost always can work with more than one user at a time

modem	"modulator-demodulator"--a hardware device that allows a computer to send or receive data over telephone lines
monitor	CRT
mouse	a device which moves the cursor around the TV screen; when the device is moved on the desk, the cursor moves
natural language	English, Japanese, etc., in contrast to artificial (programming) language
natural language interface	a computer program that uses English words for the commands; usually a small set of words and limited syntax are required
network	electronically linked computers that can communicate with each other by phone lines, other wires, or radio or TV signals, without using modems
online	when a computer is connected to some other device through phone lines or other wires
operating system	software that controls computer hardware, e.g., manages files, gets keystrokes on the screen, etc.
parameter	a variable; many computer programs work by having the user select from a set of choices before the processing starts, e.g., setting a margin at a certain column
parsing	analysis of syntax, either of a natural language or programming language
PASCAL	a programming language, often used for introductory instruction; known for its hierarchical syntax.
peripheral	physical device, such as a terminal or printer, linked to a computer
personal computer	(PC) informal name for a relatively cheap microcomputer
PILOT	an authoring language which has been implemented on many microcomputers
PLATO	an authoring system, used in several CAI systems, developed

GLOSSARY

by Control Data

printout | a text printed by a computer

program | a series of instructions, usually written in a special, artificial language (e.g., BASIC)

proportional spacing | a printing system that makes "l" narrow than "w," rather than leaving the same width for each character; this text is proportionally spaced

RAM | random access memory, information stored in a computer which can be changed by the user's program; it is not saved when the computer is turned off, but may be transferred to a disk, tape, or other mass storage device

readability formulas | efforts to translate features such as word and sentence lengths into an index of how hard a text is to read

ROM | read-only memory, information permanently stored in a computer; it cannot be changed

RSVP | series of programs written by Anadam, and others (q.v.)

screen | CRT

screen editor | a program which shows information a whole screenful at a time, instead of one line at a time; also called "display-oriented," as opposed to "line-oriented"

scrolling | a word processing command to change the part of a text which appears on a screen

search | a word processor instruction to find a specified string of letters or word(s) in a text, and to have the cursor stop when it gets there

split screen | an environment wherein different parts of TV image are marked off so that different parts of a text or texts may be displayed simultaneously

STYLE | one program on WRITER'S WORKBENCH

terminal | a device which is linked to a central processing unit, generally by phone lines or electric wires; most allow input (through a keyboard) and output (through a TV screen or printer)

text editor
a program designed to create text; usually optimized for writing computer programs rather than ordinary prose; usually display-oriented rather than line-oriented

text feedback
information such as average word length, number of prepositions, etc., which a some programs give to the user after or while they are running

text formatter
a program that obeys embedded commands to make printed copy look different from onscreen copy; e.g., @index[Churchill] would create an index entry for the word "Churchill"

text processor
a program designed to create and format text; sometimes these are optimized for writing computer programs, sometimes for ordinary prose

software
computer programs, including operating systems, compilers, and application programs such as word processors

spelling checker
a lexicon and program; the program checks the words in the text to see if they are in the lexicon; non-words (presumed to be typographical or spelling errors) are listed or highlighted on the screen

spelling corrector
a spelling checker that allows one to fix the errors, e.g., by replacing "adn" with "and", within the program, without having to load the text into one's word processor

STORY MAKER
program written by A. Rubin and others (q.v.)

string
a series of letters, numbers, blanks, or punctuation marks

TUTOR
an authoring language used in the PLATO system

UNIX
an operating system available on many microcomputers, written by Bell Labs

"user-friendly"
the general idea that a computer and its programs should present instructions explicitly and clearly, in non-technical terms, so that beginners can get started easily

VDT
Video Display Terminal, a cathode ray tube (CRT) and keyboard linked to a computer; describes the kind of

GLOSSARY

hardware available in many newspapers

WANDAH   programs written by R. Von Blum and others (q.v.)

window   a. part of a text which is visible on screen; b. part of the screen set off for special purposes

word processor   (WP) a program that facilitates the entry and editing of text; the phrase is also used to include the computer which runs the program

WORDSTAR   a word processing program available for most microcomputers; written by MicroPro, Inc.

wordwrap/wraparound   a feature of most word processing programs that allows typing to go on without inserting a carriage return at the end of a line

WP   see word processor

WRITER'S WORKBENCH programs written by Frase, Cherry and others (q.v.)

Index

About the Compilers

PAULA REED NANCARROW, formerly a Teaching Associate and FIPSE Research Assistant at the University of Minnesota, is currently Assistant Professor of English at Wheaton College in Wheaton, Illinois. She has contributed articles to *New Directions in Composition Research* and *Dictionary of Literary Biography*.

DONALD ROSS is Associate Professor of English and Composition at the University of Minnesota and Secretary of the Association for Computers in the Humanities. His articles have appeared in *PMLA*, *Style*, and a wide variety of periodicals concerned with computers and the analysis of language and linguistics.

LILLIAN BRIDWELL is Assistant Professor of English and Composition at the University of Minnesota. She has published numerous articles on the composing processes of student and professional writers and is the co-editor of *New Directions in Composition Research*.